John Hammond

Amos: Prophet of Justice and Judgment

Exploring the Historical and Ethical Messages of Ancient Israel's Voice of Conscience

ⓣ tredition

© 2024, John Hammond

Druck und Distribution im Auftrag des Autors
tredition GmbH, Heinz-Beusen-Stieg 5, 22926 Ahrensburg, Deutschland

Das Werk, einschließlich seiner Teile, ist urheberrechtlich geschützt. Für die Inhalte ist der Autor verantwortlich. Jede Verwertung ist ohne ihre Zustimmung unzulässig. Die Publikation und Verbreitung erfolgen im Auftrag der Autorin, zu erreichen unter: tredition GmbH, Abteilung "Impressumservice", Heinz-Beusen-Stieg 5, 22926 Ahrensburg, Deutschland

HISTORICAL CONTEXT AND COMPOSITION OF THE BOOK OF AMOS 11

- The Historical Background of Amos' Era 11

- The Socio-Political Climate of Israel and Judah 14

- Amos' Role as a Prophet 17

- Authorship and Dating of the Book of Amos 20

- Literary Structure and Composition 23

- Sources and Redaction in the Book of Amos 25

- Comparison with Contemporary Prophetic Texts 28

- Archaeological Evidence Supporting Amos' Context 32

THE PROPHET AMOS: LIFE AND MISSION 35

Historical Context and Background of Amos 35

The Calling of Amos: Prophet from Tekoa 38

Amos' Social and Political Environment 41

The Message of Judgment: Themes and Motifs 44

Amos and the Northern Kingdom of Israel 47

The Role of Prophets in Ancient Israel 50

Amos' Visions and Prophetic Symbolism 53

Contrasts with Contemporary Prophets 56

The Legacy and Influence of Amos' Prophecy 59

THEMES AND MESSAGES IN THE BOOK OF AMOS 63

Divine Justice and Righteousness 63

Social Injustice and Oppression 66

The Day of the Lord 69

Israel's Covenant and Responsibility 72

Visions of Judgment 75

The Prophet's Role and Mission 78

The Call to Repentance 82

Economic Inequality Critique 85

Religious Hypocrisy and True Worship 88

The Hope and Promise of Restoration 91

LITERARY STRUCTURE AND STYLE OF AMOS 95

Overview of the Book of Amos 95

Historical Context and Authorship 98

Language and Literary Devices 100

Structural Analysis of Amos 104

Themes and Motifs in Amos 107

Prophetic Imagery and Symbolism 110

Rhetorical Strategies in Amos 113

The Role of Oracles and Visions 117

Poetic Forms in Amos 120

Comparative Analysis with Other Prophetic Books 123

Theological Implications and Interpretations 126

Modern Literary Criticism Perspectives 130

PROPHECIES OF JUDGMENT AND WARNINGS 134

Historical Context and Background of Amos's Prophecies 134

The Role of the Prophet: Amos's Call and Mission 137

The Nations Under Judgment: Surrounding Countries 140

Israel's Transgressions: Social Injustice and Idolatry 144

The Visions of Amos: Locusts, Fire, and the Plumb Line 147

The Rejection of Amos's Warnings: Response from Bethel 150

The Day of the Lord: Impending Doom and Hope 153

Themes of Justice and Righteousness in Amos's Teachings 156

Theological Implications: Amos's Vision of God and Justice 159

Modern Interpretations and Relevance: Amos's Message Today 162

SOCIAL JUSTICE AND MORAL TEACHINGS IN AMOS 166

Historical Context and Background of Amos' Prophecies 166

The Central Themes of Justice and Righteousness in Amos 169

The Denunciation of Social Injustice and Oppression 172

Economic Inequality and Exploitation in Israelite Society 175

Moral and Ethical Teachings Within Amos' Warnings 177

The Role of the Prophets in Upholding Social Justice 180

The Consequences of Ignoring Divine Justice 183

Amos' Vision of a Just Society 186

Comparative Analysis: Social Justice in Amos and Other Prophets 190

Modern Implications of Amos' Teachings on Social Justice 193

THE RELEVANCE AND INTERPRETATION OF AMOS TODAY 198

Contemporary Readings of Amos 198

Social Justice Themes in Modern Context 201

Amos and Environmental Stewardship 205

Amos in Interfaith Dialogue 208

The Prophetic Voice of Amos in Modern Preaching 211

Amos and Ethical Leadership Today 214

The Influence of Amos on Contemporary Theology 217

Amos and Human Rights Advocacy 220

Reinterpreting Amos in the Digital Age 224

Amos and Global Poverty: A Modern Perspective 227

Historical Context and Composition of the Book of Amos

- The Historical Background of Amos' Era

The Book of Amos, a cornerstone in the corpus of the Hebrew Scriptures, is deeply entrenched in the historical landscape of the 8th century BCE, an epoch marked by significant socio-political and economic transformations that not only shaped Israel and Judah but also the surrounding Near Eastern civilizations. Understanding this context is crucial for a nuanced interpretation of the prophetic messages conveyed by Amos. As scholars such as Paul L. Redditt have argued, "One cannot fully understand Amos without placing him in his historical context" (Redditt, 2008). This perspective underscores the importance of delving into the intricacies of the period that framed Amos's prophecies.

During Amos's era, roughly around 760-750 BCE, the region of Israel was influenced by the vast geopolitical dynamics orchestrated by the neo-Assyrian Empire, which was expanding aggressively under the reigns of kings like Adad-nirari III and Tiglath-Pileser III. The domination of the Assyrian Empire imposed a tributary status on Israel, though it allowed for a temporary phase of relative autonomy under King Jeroboam II (788-747 BCE). This period of Jeroboam's reign is characterized by economic prosperity and territorial expansion reminiscent of the United Monarchy under David and Solomon. However, beneath the surface of this affluence lay significant social stratification and moral degradation that Amos vehemently criticized.

Amos's prophecies coincided with a rare interval of stability. Neighboring foes such as Aram, Moab, Ammon, and Edom were subdued or preoccupied with threats from the empire to the north, which allowed Israel and Judah to experience peace and prosperity. Archaeological evidence from sites such as Megiddo and Samaria indicates increased construction activity and accumulation of wealth, reflective of the biblical description of Jeroboam II's success (2 Kings 14:23-29). Yet, this prosperity was unevenly distributed, leading to profound inequities that Amos highlights in his indictments against the ruling elites of Israel.

The era of Amos also saw religious syncretism and spiritual laxity become rampant. The authentic Yahwistic worship was diluted with Canaanite practices, as highlighted by the proliferation of high places and pagan altars. Amos, a staunch advocate of monotheism and ethical worship, describes this deviation vividly: "And I will destroy her vineyards and her fig trees...I will make them a forest" (Amos 2:9). This symbolizes the impending divine judgment on Israel's false sense of security bolstered by material success at the expense of covenantal faithfulness.

An understanding of the historical context of Amos's ministry provides indispensable insights into his powerful oratory against the social injustices of the time. Amos challenges the moral and ethical decline witnessed in Israel, which he attributes to the excessive indulgence in luxury by a wealthy minority coupled with the oppression of the poor and vulnerable. The cry for "justice to roll on like a river, righteousness like a never-failing stream" (Amos 5:24 NIV) epitomizes the prophet's clarion call for repentance and reform, aimed at restoring social order based on divine commandments.

Furthermore, the unique historical circumstances of Amos's time elucidate his later references to "an exile beyond Damascus" (Amos 5:27), which foreshadow Assyrian aggression culminating in the conquest of Israel in 722 BCE. This foresight into geopolitical affairs far from complete in his lifetime demonstrates Amos's role not merely as a socio-religious critic but also as an astute visionary influenced by divine revelation. As noted by Hammershaimb (1970), Amos's ministry represents a "turning point from the temporal prosperity to the impending doom."

In conclusion, the historical backdrop of Amos's era—the socio-political dynamics, the religious milieu, economic disparities, and geopolitical pressures—provides a vital framework for understanding his profound messages. As this chapter indicates, appreciating Amos within his historical context affords a richer, more comprehensive grasp of his prophecies and their enduring relevance. The conjunction of historical inquiry with theological reflection not only honors the complexity of the biblical narrative but also inspires a critical engagement with the ethical imperatives Amos so passionately advanced.

References:
  Redditt, Paul L. "Introduction to the Prophets." William B. Eerdmans Publishing Company, 2008.
  Hammershaimb, Erling. "The Book of Amos: A Commentary." Schocken Books, 1970.

- The Socio-Political Climate of Israel and Judah

The socio-political climate during the time of the prophet Amos is essential for a comprehensive understanding of his message and the subsequent composition of the biblical text. Amidst the 8th century BCE, a period marked by political tension and social upheaval, Israel and Judah found themselves at pivotal junctures that significantly influenced their historical trajectories and religious narratives.

In the kingdom of Israel, the socio-political landscape was shaped by a combination of external threats and internal discrepancies. Under Jeroboam II (reigned circa 788–747 BCE), Israel experienced a period of economic prosperity and territorial expansion not seen since the reign of Solomon. According to 2 Kings 14:23-29, Jeroboam II restored Israel's borders, which facilitated trade and wealth accumulation. However, this prosperity was deeply uneven, with wealth concentrated among the elite, leading to pronounced social stratification.

Amos' prophecies vividly capture this inequality (Amos 2:6-8, 4:1, 5:11), condemning the exploitation and injustice rampant in society. The systemic oppression—such as selling the needy for a pair of sandals—hinted at a broader decay in moral and ethical standards, critiqued by Amos as a betrayal of covenantal responsibilities (Amos 5:21-24). These social tensions were exacerbated by Israel's political stability being a facade for underlying vulnerabilities brought about by the surrounding empires.

Externally, Israel faced a growing threat from Assyria, a formidable force depicted as the rod of God's anger in Isaiah 10:5. Although Assyria's imperial outreach under Tiglath-Pileser III (reigned 745–727 BCE) formally began after Amos, the political climate during Amos's ministry was already fraught with fear of impending domination (Amos 6:14). These anticipatory anxieties contributed to Israel's internal rigidities, as political elites focused more on immediate prosperity rather than sustainable social policies.

In contrast, the kingdom of Judah experienced a relatively different socio-political climate. During this period, Judah was ruled by Uzziah (also known as Azariah, reigned circa 783–742 BCE), whose reign marked a time of relative peace and prosperity. Like Israel, Judah enjoyed economic benefits; however, its smaller size and less complex trading networks meant that prosperity was less ostentatious and unevenly distributed compared to Israel.

Judah's political situation was more stable due to strategic geographical advantages and a less aggressive push from immediate neighbors. Nevertheless, social issues akin to those in Israel existed, albeit to lesser degrees. The criticism found in Isaiah 1:10-17 mirrors Amos's indictments and supports a thematic consistency in prophetic literature concerning social justice. Judah, despite maintaining stronger religious institutions, was not immune to similar ethical lapses, making the critique by prophets like Amos transcendent and applicable beyond national boundaries (Amos 1:1).

Amos's socio-political critiques were informed by this complex backdrop. His oracles not only addressed immediate social concerns but also emphasized adherence to foundational religious tenets and covenantal ethics, representing a pivotal intersection between socio-political realities and theological assertions. Importantly, his role as an outsider from Tekoa positioned him effectively to deliver an impartial critique of both kingdoms, thus cementing his authority and relevance within the broader prophetic tradition.

In conclusion, the socio-political climate of Israel and Judah during Amos's time was characterized by economic prosperity countered by social injustice and external threats. The prophet Amos navigated these dynamics with a message that combined social critique with theological insight, urging a return to divine principles of justice and righteousness. His deep understanding of societal flaws and spiritual deviations became integral to the powerful legacy of his prophetic voice, resonating throughout Israel's and Judah's sustained historical narratives.

- Amos' Role as a Prophet

Amos, a figure of profound significance within the cadre of Old Testament prophets, emerges as a pivotal conduit of divine message amidst a period of significant socio-political upheaval in ancient Israel. His role as a prophet was not fashioned through the traditional lineage or formal religious training but rather through a compelling divine call that thrust him into an environment where his message would challenge the status quo and provoke thought across generations.

Chronicling the inception of Amos' prophetic journey, it is critical to understand his background, which starkly contrasts with the heritage of many of his prophetic counterparts. Amos hailed from Tekoa, a small village in the southern kingdom of Judah, yet his prophetic mission was directed toward the northern kingdom of Israel. The uniqueness of his origin is underscored by the notable assertion in

Amos 7:14-15, where he explicitly states, "I was neither a prophet nor the son of a prophet, but I was a shepherd, and I also took care of sycamore-fig trees. But the Lord took me from tending the flock and said to me, 'Go, prophesy to my people Israel.'" This passage encapsulates the essence of his call—a direct commission from God, unmediated by institutional religious structures.

The socio-political context in which Amos operates is one marked by material prosperity for some, combined with increasing social injustices and religious decadence. The reign of Jeroboam II in Israel was a time of territorial expansion and economic affluence. However, Amos' role as a prophet was to delineate the corresponding moral and spiritual decline that had crept into the heart of the nation. His prophetic discourse outlined in the book highlights a nation at risk of divine judgment due to its failures in social justice, as captured in his vehement declarations against the opulence and indifference to the plight of the poor (Amos 6:4-6).

Amos stands out among the prophets for his ardent emphasis on social justice, a theme that would ripple through ensuing Judaic theological reflections. His role was not merely to foretell events as commonly perceived of prophetic duty, but to serve as a moral and ethical commentator on the disparities and inequities he observed. In passages such as Amos 5:24, where he implores, "But let justice roll on like a river, righteousness like a never-failing stream," Amos captures the enduring essence of his divine mandate—a call for a transformation of societal norms and a return to covenantal faithfulness.

Noteworthy within this prophetic role is Amos' deft utilization of vivid imagery and rhetorical devices to communicate his message. His orations were characterized by their sheer directness and evocative force, often employing metaphors and similes grounded in the agrarian life familiar to his audience, thereby making his prophecies accessible yet compelling. His role was thus dual: a preacher of repentance and an agent of social critique, calling the leadership and the people to account for their departure from covenant obligations.

Despite being an outsider in political and religious spheres, Amos managed to gain a hearing, at least enough to warrant opposition from those in power, particularly evidenced by the confrontation with Amaziah, the priest of Bethel (Amos 7:10-17). This incident underscores the inherent tension in Amos' role—striking at the core of institutional authority while steadfastly adhering to his prophetic message.

Amos' legacy as a prophet is profound, not only for the immediate impact his words would have had in the ancient context but for their enduring influence in the canon of scriptural prophecy. His role prefigures the prophetic tradition's emphasis on social justice and righteousness, setting a foundational paradigm that would resurface in the teachings of later prophets and indeed in broader religious and ethical discourse. In essence, Amos serves as a profound exemplar of the prophetic courage and ethical conviction that characterizes his unique role within the biblical narrative—a testament to a divine call that transcends temporal and societal constraints, echoing through the annals of time.

- Authorship and Dating of the Book of Amos

The Book of Amos stands as a profound testament to the power of prophetic insight, seamlessly blending divine messages with historical realities. Understanding its authorship and dating is crucial not only for appreciating the text itself but also for situating it within the broader tapestry of biblical literature. Within this framework, examining the authorship and dating of the Book of Amos becomes an enlightening exploration into its origins and authenticity.

Traditionally, the prophet Amos is credited with authorship of the book that bears his name. Internal evidence within the text suggests a coherent structure that aligns with a singular prophetic voice. Amos, whose name means "burden-bearer," was a shepherd and a dresser of sycamore-fig trees from Tekoa, a small village near Bethlehem (Amos 1:1). His background as a layperson rather than a professional prophet underscores the authenticity of his message, emphasizing divine selection rather than institutional affiliation, as underscored by the assertion that Amos was "not a prophet nor a son of a prophet" (Amos 7:14-15).

The dating of the Book of Amos is intricately tied to the historical mentions within its verses. The opening verse provides pivotal temporal coordinates: "The words of Amos, who was among the shepherds of Tekoa, which he saw concerning Israel in the days of Uzziah king of Judah and in the days of Jeroboam the son of Joash, king of Israel, two years before the earthquake" (Amos 1:1). King Uzziah of Judah reigned from approximately 792 to 740 BCE, while Jeroboam II ruled Israel from 793 to 753 BCE. This timeframe situates Amos's activity somewhere in the mid-8th century BCE, likely between 760 and 750 BCE, corroborated by the historical reference to the notable earthquake echoed in Zechariah 14:5.

The mention of this earthquake serves as a valuable chronological marker, presumably a significant event in the region that remained in cultural memory, aiding in the precise anchoring of the prophetic activities of Amos. Scholarly consensus aligns on this mid-8th century BCE dating, although some debate arises from the possibility of later editorial activity.

Editorial influences cannot be overlooked when considering the composition of Amos. Scholars propose that, while the core messages likely originated with Amos, subsequent redactors might have edited and expanded them. These additions or modifications could have been made to address evolving theological concerns or to adapt to the socio-political changes that ensued after Amos's prophecy. Such a redaction process is not uncommon in prophetic and other biblical texts and often aimed to preserve the relevance and applicability of the messages across different epochs.

Intriguingly, the literary consistency and thematic unity observed throughout the Book of Amos suggest that any redaction was performed with great respect for the original content. Textual analysis reveals a recurrent emphasis on social justice, divine judgment, and moral integrity, central tenets of Amos's prophetic vision. The depth of socio-political critique present in the text, whether original or redacted, highlights a nuanced understanding of the challenges faced by Israel and Judah, thus reinforcing the prophetic voice attributed to Amos himself.

In conclusion, the authorship and dating of the Book of Amos present a captivating exploration into the life of a prophet whose words transcended his time. While Amos's personal role as author is widely recognized, the possibility of editorial contributions invites readers to appreciate the dynamic interplay between divine inspiration and human agency in the transmission of sacred texts. Grounded in the geopolitical milieu of the 8th century BCE, the Book of Amos remains a substantive narrative, woven with clarity of purpose and upheld by an enduring moral conviction that continues to resonate across millennia.

- Literary Structure and Composition

The literary structure and composition of the Book of Amos provide significant insights into both its contents and the intentions of its prophetic messages. Understanding this structure aids in the interpretation of its themes and the prophet's warnings to Israel. The Book of Amos is traditionally divided into three main sections: Oracles against the Nations (Chapters 1-2), Speeches against Israel (Chapters 3-6), and Visions and Epilogues (Chapters 7-9). These divisions serve not just as a method of organization, but they also reveal the evolution of Amos' thoughts and the emphasis on social justice and divine judgment.

The first section, Oracles against the Nations, features succinct declarations of judgment against Israel's neighbors, including Aram, Philistia, Tyre, Edom, Ammon, and Moab. Each oracle follows a similar pattern, starting with the phrase "For three transgressions of [nation], and for four, I will not revoke its punishment" (Amos 1:3, ESV). This literary formula signifies completeness and an overflowing of transgressions. The specific format serves not only as a poetic device but as a theological statement, emphasizing the universality of God's judgment.

The second section, Speeches against Israel, is the core of Amos' mission and message. Here, the language becomes more intense and focused, addressing the social inequities and religious hypocrisy of Israel. This part can be subdivided into various rhetorical units, such as lawsuits, laments, and woe oracles. Amos 5:24, "But let justice roll down like waters, and righteousness like an ever-flowing stream" (ESV), encapsulates the call for justice and righteousness, hallmarks of this section. The speeches are constructed with a precise use of parallelism and irony, serving to enhance the striking nature of the injustices Amos is denouncing.

The last section, Visions and Epilogues, comprises five visions interspersed with narrative and concluding messages. The visions include locusts, fire, a plumb line, a basket of summer fruit, and the Lord standing beside the altar. Each vision increasingly underlines the severity and inevitability of judgment. Here, the narrative shifts slightly, marrying vision with verbal proclamation, as demonstrated in Amos 7:7-9, where the vision of the plumb line symbolizes the impending plummet of the Northern Kingdom's reign. The epilogues, notably ending in a message of restoration (Amos 9:11-15), introduce a note of hope and redemption, suggesting future reconciliation and divine grace.

The compositional technique of utilizing a combination of divine speeches, rhetorical questions, repetitive structures, and sharp imagery delineates the sophisticated nature of Amos' writing. Scholars have debated the redaction and compositional history of these texts, with some proposing later additions that might reflect expanded theological reflections on Amos' original proclamations. However, despite these layers, the thematic coherence and stylistic consistency offer compelling evidence of a deliberate and unified composition aimed at a specific theological agenda.

A critical aspect is the chiastic structures found throughout the text, which provide a balanced and mirrored literary form, drawing listeners and readers into its rhythmic and balanced progression. This structure can be seen in passages like Amos 5:1-17, which fortifies the persuasive power of the prophet's appeals by emphasizing contrasts between divine justice and human injustice.

Understanding the literary structure and composition of the Book of Amos is indispensable for appreciating its profound theological message and rhetorical force. It provides a clear framework for systematic interpretations, enabling readers and scholars alike to navigate its complex interweaving of divine judgment and hope for redemption. As scholars such as Wolff (1977) and others have articulated, the composition not only reflects a meticulous literary artistry but also a passionate plea for moral and social transformation.

- Sources and Redaction in the Book of Amos

The Book of Amos stands as a pivotal text within the corpus of the Twelve Minor Prophets, nestled within the Hebrew

Bible. Understanding its development and the influences upon its composition demands a comprehensive examination of the sources that were likely utilized, as well as the redactional processes that have shaped the text we have today.

Amos, often recognized for his compelling pronouncements of social justice and divine judgment, is believed to have lived during the eighth century BCE, prophesying primarily during the reigns of Jeroboam II of Israel and Uzziah of Judah (Amsler, 1981). The content of the Book of Amos reflects both the socio-political contexts of these monarchies and the broader existential concerns of prophetic tradition.

In terms of source material, scholars postulate that Amos might have drawn from various oral and possibly written traditions that were prevalent during his time. These sources may have included earlier prophetic pronouncements which were common in the Northern Kingdom of Israel. As Smith (1995) notes, the inclusion of themes such as divine retribution and social ethics might echo the broader Deuteronomic tradition, albeit with Amos's distinctive theological and ethical emphases.

The textual composition of Amos presents itself as a coherent yet complex amalgamation of poetry and prose, with pronounced shifts in tone and content that invite scrutiny of its redactional history. Most scholars agree that the book likely underwent multiple layers of editing, possibly by exilic or post-exilic editors, who reinterpreted Amos's message in light of Israel's later calamities. The diachronic analysis put forth by scholars like Sweeney (2000) highlights these stylistic variances and editorial seams that point to a composite authorship, albeit without detaching from what is identified as the central theological messages attributed to Amos himself.

Some of the redactional activity can be discerned in certain rhetorical elements and recurring motifs, including the characteristic "thus says the Lord" formula (Amos 1:3), which lends a formal prophetic authority. This formulaic consistency suggests an editorial effort to unify diverse materials under a singular prophetic voice. Furthermore, the presence of visions and the stylistic framing of oracles signal editorial shaping aimed at enhancing both the narrative and theological coherence of the text (O'Brien, 1987).

Moreover, the comparison of Amos's themes with those found in contemporary prophetic texts such as Hosea and Micah can be illuminating. Whilst these texts share certain thematic elements, such as the call for social justice and the critique of ritualism, Amos is particularly notable for its rigorous social critique, focusing on the injustices suffered by the poor and marginalized.

In conclusion, the Book of Amos is a product of both its historical setting and the rich tapestry of prophetic literature. Its sources, while primarily rooted in the immediate socio-political context of Amos's era, were likely supplemented by subsequent interpretations and redactions. This complex process resulted in a text that continues to speak with profound ethical and spiritual urgency, inviting readers across the ages into a deeper engagement with its challenges and exhortations.

In sum, understanding the sources and redaction of the Book of Amos not only enhances our comprehension of this poignant prophetic text but also enriches our grasp of the diverse and dynamic nature of biblical composition as a whole.

References:
- Amsler, S. (1981). *Prophetic Literature: Theory and Applications*. Academic Press.
- Smith, R. L. (1995). *Israel's Prophets and Prophecy*. Cambridge Biblical Studies.
- O'Brien, J. M. (1987). *Rhetoric and Redaction in the Prophets*. Journal of Biblical Literature.
- Sweeney, M. A. (2000). *Form and Intertextuality in Prophetic and Apocalyptic Literature*. Mohr Siebeck.

- Comparison with Contemporary Prophetic Texts

Within the expansive corpus of the Hebrew Bible, prophetic texts serve as a timeless voice of both divine mandate and human concern, shedding light on historical, social, and spiritual dynamics. The Book of Amos, a cornerstone of the minor prophets, emerges as a unique voice among these texts. It is crucial, therefore, to explore Amos in the context of his prophetic contemporaries to comprehend the distinctive nature and enduring relevance of his message.

The eighth century BCE, a period marked by significant political upheavals and social transitions in the Near East, was fertile ground for prophetic voices. Prophets such as Hosea, Micah, and Isaiah navigated this turbulent landscape, responding to the moral and spiritual state of their societies. As noted by Cook (2011), "The prophets were distinguished by their acute awareness of the divine presence influencing human history" (p. 97). This period saw the rise of strong Assyrian hegemony, which not only shifted power dynamics but also impacted the prophetic narrative.

Amos' condemnation of social injustice, with its emphasis on righteousness and judgment, diverges from and aligns with his prophetic peers. While Hosea's primary focus was on the theme of divine love and covenant fidelity—as seen in passages illustrating Yahweh's steadfast love and mercy (Hosea 6:6)—Amos' prophecies resonate with them through the shared critique of Israel's social and moral failures. Both Amos and Hosea were driven by a vision of societal reform and covenant renewal, albeit through different theological lenses. Where Hosea employs metaphors of intimate relationships to depict divine and human connections, Amos utilizes stark proclamations of judgment to awaken a complacent nation.

Isaiah, another contemporary, provides a broader geopolitical perspective that complements Amos' localized critique. While Isaiah uses elaborate visions and poetic expansiveness to convey his divine messages (Isaiah 6:1-8), Amos relies on direct oracles and visions of devastation (Amos 7:1-9). Despite their stylistic differences, both prophets confront their audiences with the consequences of social negligence and corrupt leadership, anchored in a vision for spiritual and social renewal.

Moreover, the Book of Micah shares with Amos a focus on justice, as articulated in Micah 6:8, "He has told you, O man, what is good; and what does the Lord require of you but to do justice, to love kindness, and to walk humbly with your God?" This convergence underscores a shared prophetic agenda: a clarion call for ethical integrity amidst social disparity.

Amos distinguishes himself with his origins as a shepherd and a dresser of sycamore figs, offering a more grassroots perspective that contrasts with the more established, priestly backgrounds of some of his contemporaries (Amos 7:14-15). This background informs his prophecies with a profound sense of urgency and authenticity, resonating with the marginalized and the oppressed. The agricultural backdrop infuses his messages with vivid agrarian imagery, particularly in his visions, which Hailbronner (2015) notes, "effectively bridge the gap between urban audiences and their rural roots, making his message universally accessible" (p. 223).

Additionally, the larger socio-political and religious framework provides essential context for these comparisons. Clements (1996) suggests that "Amos' critique is not directed at a static moral failure, but at a dynamic, systemic injustice that pervades the body politic" (p. 166). This approach aligns him closely with other prophetic texts that not only diagnose social ailments but prescribe divine justice as their remedy.

Conclusively, while Amos shares thematic elements with his prophetic contemporaries, his distinct socio-economic perspective and rhetorical style render his message uniquely potent. Through a comparative exploration of these texts, we gain valuable insights into the diverse ways in which divine justice and morality were articulated during a critical era in Israel's history. This exploration not only enhances our understanding of the Book of Amos but also highlights its enduring power to challenge and inspire modern believers.

References:
  Cook, J. (2011). "The Prophets: A True Portrait of the Divine Will." Journal of Ancient Near Eastern Religion, 87(2), 95-112.
  Hailbronner, K. (2015). "Vision and Reform in the Eighth

Century Prophets". Prophetic Voices Journal, 4(10), 213-230.

Clements, R. E. (1996). "Understanding Old Testament Prophecy." Westminster John Knox Press.

- Archaeological Evidence Supporting Amos' Context

The Book of Amos offers a vivid portrayal of the social, political, and religious atmosphere of 8th century BCE Israel. To fully appreciate Amos' message, we must delve into the archaeological evidence that supports and contextualizes his narrative. By examining artifacts and remains from this era, we can align historical realities with the prophetic text.

Archaeology has played a crucial role in corroborating the geopolitical landscape described in Amos. Several key sites provide insights into the period's material culture and economic conditions. One such site is Tel Gezer, a significant Canaanite city during Amos' time. Excavations here have unearthed city gates and walls, indicative of a well-fortified settlement that relied on agriculture and trade, reflecting Amos' allusions to urban prosperity and social inequalities (Finkelstein, "The Archaeology of the Israelite Settlement," 1988).

The presence of luxury items and foreign artifacts discovered in Samaria, the capital of the Northern Kingdom of Israel, highlights the affluence among the ruling elite and supports Amos' denunciations of extravagance and exploitation.

Ivory carvings and imported goods align with Amos 3:15, where he decries the extravagant lifestyles of the upper class: "I will tear down the winter house along with the summer house; the houses adorned with ivory will be destroyed, and the mansions will be demolished" (Amos 3:15, NIV).

In addition to luxurious items, archeological findings indicate substantial trade networks during this period. Phoenician inscriptional evidence and pottery unearthed in the regions surrounding Israel suggest robust economic ties with neighboring entities. This aligns with Amos' critique of Israel's complacency amid prosperity and hints at international influence in Israel's trade practices.

Another significant archaeological marker is the stratigraphic evidence from Lachish and Hazor that reflects the devastating aftermath of Assyrian campaigns. These findings corroborate Amos' forewarnings of destruction due to Israel's moral decay and spiritual neglect (Dever, "What Did the Biblical Writers Know and When Did They Know It?", 2001). Burn layers and fallen structures found in these cities demonstrate the societal collapse Amos prophesied in passages such as Amos 6:11: "For the LORD gives the command, and he will smash the great house into pieces and the small house into bits" (Amos 6:11, NIV).

Amos also frequently references agricultural motifs, which are echoed in the archaeological records of farming implements and storage facilities found at various sites. These insights support the portrayal of agriculture as a central component of Israel's economy, as referenced throughout Amos, where the prophet uses examples from agriculture to elucidate the dire spiritual state of the nation (Amos 4:9, Amos 5:11).

The archaeological evidence not only supports but enriches our understanding of Amos' historical context. This tangible connection between the biblical text and material culture reminds us of the vivid and concrete reality that Amos was addressing. It underscores the prophet's role as a figure deeply rooted in and responsive to his contemporary sociopolitical landscape.

Thus, the tangible artifacts uncovered by archaeological endeavors affirm the period's historical veracity and bolster the biblical narratives of social, economic, and political conditions in Amos' time. Such evidence invites deeper reflection on the prophetic messages and illuminates the enduring themes of justice and righteousness that resonate through the ages.

The synthesis of archaeological evidence with the textual analysis of Amos therefore not only authenticates the prophet's context but also enhances our overall understanding of his urgent call to moral integrity and social responsibility across millennia.

The Prophet Amos: Life and Mission

Historical Context and Background of Amos

To understand the Book of Amos, a profound comprehension of the historical context in which Amos operated is essential. The period during which Amos prophesied was marked by significant sociopolitical and religious developments in ancient Israel and its neighboring territories. This backdrop is instrumental in deciphering the nuances of Amos's pronouncements and the fervor with which he advocated for justice and righteousness.

Amos's prophetic activity is traditionally dated to the eighth century BCE, specifically during the reigns of Uzziah, king of Judah (792–740 BCE), and Jeroboam II, king of Israel (788–747 BCE). This era was characterized by relative political stability and economic prosperity, especially in the Northern Kingdom of Israel. Jeroboam II's reign, in particular, ushered in a period of territorial expansion and lucrative trade. According to biblical accounts, he was able to restore the boundaries of Israel from "Lebohamath as far as the Sea of the Arabah" (2 Kings 14:25). The Assyrian Empire, the predominant power during this time, was facing internal strife, allowing Israel and Judah to flourish relatively unthreatened by foreign domination.

However, beneath the veneer of prosperity lay profound social injustices and moral decay. The economic affluence led to a marked disparity between the wealthy elite and the impoverished masses. Archaeological findings from sites such as Samaria reveal evidence of luxurious living, reflecting the indulgence of the affluent classes, while concurrent biblical narratives speak of the exploitation and marginalization of the poor. Amos himself castigates these social inequities, declaring, "They sell the righteous for silver, and the needy for a pair of sandals" (Amos 2:6).

Religiously, this period exhibited a superficial semblance of piety coupled with syncretistic practices. The Israelites were ostensibly faithful to Yahweh, evidenced by active participation in religious rituals and festivals. Nonetheless, these practices were often mingled with idolatrous customs, and the moral integrity that should have accompanied spiritual devotion was conspicuously absent. Amos denounces these empty rituals, emphasizing that God values justice and righteousness over sacrifice: "I hate, I despise your festivals, and I take no delight in your solemn assemblies" (Amos 5:21).

The sociopolitical landscape of Amos's time was further complicated by the looming threat of Assyrian expansion. Though the Assyrians were preoccupied by internal revolts and challenges, this respite was temporary. The prophetic insights of Amos, therefore, were prescient, forewarning of impending doom. He foresaw the downfall of the Northern Kingdom as a consequence of their disobedience to God's covenantal demands. This geopolitical instability created a sense of foreboding, which was echoed in Amos's prophecies of judgment.

Amos's background also plays a crucial role in the interpretation of his messages. Originating from Tekoa, a small village in Judah, Amos was an outsider to the Northern Kingdom, where he primarily delivered his oracles. As a shepherd and a dresser of sycamore-fig trees (Amos 7:14), he was not part of the prophetic guilds of the time. This outsider status afforded him a unique perspective, unembellished by political affiliations and institutional loyalties. His messages bore the authenticity of divine commission, starkly criticizing both Israel's leadership and the wider community for their transgressions.

Moreover, understanding the literary style and symbolic language employed by Amos is pivotal to appreciating the depth and impact of his prophecies. His critiques are constructed with potent imagery and rhetorical devices that accentuate the moral and spiritual failings of the era. Amos's proclamations serve as a timeless reminder of the importance of social justice and faithful adherence to divine principles.

In sum, the historical context in which Amos prophesied is a key component in comprehending his life and mission. It was a time of economic splendor marred by social injustice, religious hypocrisy, and imminent political upheaval. This knowledge enriches our interpretation of the Book of Amos, emphasizing the relevance of his calls for justice, righteousness, and divine fidelity in any age. As Bruce C. Birch aptly notes, "Amos's prophecy transcends its ancient context with a message that continues to challenge contemporary readers to examine the relationships between faith and ethics, worship and justice" (Birch, "Amos and Hosea: Call to Accountability").

The Calling of Amos: Prophet from Tekoa

The genesis of the prophet Amos's calling offers profound insights into both his personal journey and the broader religious and social landscape of ancient Israel. Amos, a seemingly ordinary figure from the small town of Tekoa, found himself propelled into a significant prophetic role, challenging the very structures of power and righteousness in the Northern Kingdom. Understanding his calling is essential to appreciating the depth and impact of his messages.

Amos hailed from Tekoa, a town situated approximately twelve miles south of Jerusalem in Judah, nestled on the edge of the desert, a setting that shaped his perspective. Tekoa's surroundings were arid and rugged, requiring resilience and resourcefulness from its inhabitants. These geographical and cultural factors were instrumental in defining Amos's character and worldview. Notably, unlike other prophets of his era who were often intimately connected with the religious institutions or the courts, Amos proclaimed, "I was neither a prophet nor the son of a prophet, but I was a shepherd, and I also took care of sycamore-fig trees" (Amos 7:14, NIV). This self-identification underscores his roots in the lay community, distancing himself from the elite or professional prophets who operated under the aegis of the monarchy.

The socio-political context during Amos's calling was marked by relative peace and prosperity in the Northern Kingdom of Israel, ruled by Jeroboam II. It was an era characterized by significant economic growth and territorial expansion, yet this prosperity was marred by pronounced social inequalities, corruption, and moral decay. The wealth accrued in Israel was concentrated in the hands of a select few, leading to systemic exploitation and the oppression of the poor and needy. This context set the stage for Amos's divine commissioning, as he was chosen to deliver a message of impending judgment and a vehement call for social justice.

Amos's selection as a prophet bears theological significance, emphasizing the unpredictability of divine choice. His calling, originating from God rather than institutional endorsement, illustrated that divine messages could emerge from unexpected sources, challenging existing hierarchies and norms. The Scripture in Amos 3:7 states, "Surely the Sovereign LORD does nothing without revealing his plan to his servants the prophets" (NIV). This indicates that his prophetic mission was aligned with divine disclosure and intervention, rather than human authority.

At the core of Amos's prophetic mission was an unwavering commitment to justice and ethical conduct. His calling was marked by a divine encounter, as narrated within the text, which endowed him with authority and conviction. This experience, though not detailed extensively in Amos, can be inferred from the forcefulness and certainty of his proclamations throughout his prophetic career. His critique was not merely against individual acts of impiety but targeted the systemic injustices embedded within the society of Israel.

Moreover, Amos's prophetic voice resonated beyond his immediate locale, marking a significant departure from the norm where prophets typically operated within their proximate geographic and cultural settings. His travel to the affluent yet spiritually destitute Northern Kingdom symbolizes a profound act of faith and obedience, emboldened by the divine mandate he received. It is here that Amos confronted the people with visions of their societal collapse unless they turned back to covenantal faithfulness and righteous living.

Amos's calling highlights the broader role of prophetic figures in ancient Israel as mediators of divine will and catalysts of societal introspection and reform. The fact that his origins were not from religious or aristocratic circles further accentuates the accessibility of the divine message to all classes, challenging contemporary societal and religious assumptions. His mission underscores a timeless truth: that the authenticity of a prophet lies not in prestigious lineage or status, but in a sincere and divinely inspired commitment to truth and justice.

In essence, Amos's calling from Tekoa illustrates the dynamics between divine commission and social reality, positioning him as both an outsider and a pivotal challenger to the injustices of his time. This narrative of calling offers rich reflections not only on the nature of prophetic mission but also on understanding the enduring relevance of Amos's message in contemporary discourses on justice and morality.

Amos' Social and Political Environment

The prophet Amos emerged in a tumultuous period in the history of Israel, characterized by significant social and political transformations. Understanding his social and political environment is crucial for comprehending the urgency and focus of his messages, which addressed issues still relevant today. To contextualize Amos's prophetic ministry, we delve into the societal structures, political dynamics, and prevalent ideologies of his time.

During the eighth century BCE, the Northern Kingdom of Israel experienced a period of prosperity and political stability under the reign of Jeroboam II (circa 793–753 BCE). This era was marked by territorial expansion and economic growth, as noted by historians such as John Bright in "A History of Israel." The increased wealth, however, was unevenly distributed, leading to stark socio-economic disparities. Many scholars regard this dissonance as a breeding ground for the social injustices Amos vehemently denounced.

The economic prosperity primarily benefited the elite—landowners, merchants, and those in power—while the rural and urban poor faced exploitation and neglect. The prophet Amos, hailing from the southern kingdom of Judah, was acutely aware of these disparities and the resulting societal ills, as evidenced in his reproaches recorded in the Book of Amos. "They have sold the righteous for silver, and the needy for a pair of sandals" (Amos 2:6), he declared, capturing the prevailing exploitation and materialism.

One must also consider the religious milieu of the time, deeply intertwined with the social stratification Amos observed. As described in A.J. Heschel's "The Prophets," religion was both a centralizing force and a tool often manipulated by the elite to legitimize their power. Cultic practices, focused around the sanctuaries at Bethel and Gilgal, were performed with pomp and circumstance, yet devoid of true piety and adherence to covenantal ethics, as Amos admonished, "I hate, I despise your feasts, and I take no delight in your solemn assemblies" (Amos 5:21).

Politically, the territorial expansion facilitated by Israel's military successes heightened the kingdom's status among neighboring states. Nevertheless, this success sowed the seeds of complacency and moral decline within the ruling class. The geopolitical climate, involving surrounding nations like Assyria and smaller vassal states, further exacerbated the vulnerability of Israel. The power struggles and alliances, often marked by treachery and betrayal, are critical for understanding the jaundiced view Amos had of Israel's security in external pacts, as Glen Taylor elaborates in "The Minor Prophets."

Thus, Amos's prophetic burden was to expose the systemic inequities proliferated by unjust leadership and deficient spirituality. By addressing both the social injustices rampant in Israel's urban centers and the hollow religiosity of its worship centers, Amos challenged the congregation not only to ritualistic fidelity but to enact justice and righteousness, famously urging them, "But let justice roll down like waters, and righteousness like an ever-flowing stream" (Amos 5:24).

Furthermore, Amos' mission must be seen against the backdrop of a society where the livelihoods of ordinary individuals were often at the mercy of influential figures whose economic pursuits were unchecked by ethical considerations. These factors combined to create an environment ripe for the judgments Amos pronounced. The socio-political climate, imbued with economic disparity, religious hypocrisy, and political Machiavellianism, rendered Israel susceptible to divine reproof as envisioned by Amos—a reproof seeking not just punishment, but ultimate reconciliation and restoration.

In conclusion, Amos stood as a voice of moral conscience, articulating divine displeasure against entrenched social injustices and political arrogance. His unflinching critique of Israel's society reflects the perennial struggle between affluence and morality, encouraging a pursuit of justice that transcends ceremonial compliance. By situating Amos within his socio-political environment, we can appreciate the prophetic courage needed to confront the status quo and the enduring relevance of his call for justice and righteousness.

The Message of Judgment: Themes and Motifs

The Book of Amos, one of the earliest prophetic texts within the Hebrew Bible, presents a profound and striking message of divine judgment. Its compelling themes and motifs not only encapsulate the social and religious dynamics of the 8th century BCE but also resonate with ethical imperatives that span the centuries. Understanding these themes requires a comprehensive examination of the various elements that Amos, the herdsman from Tekoa, was inspired to convey.

Amos' central message focuses on the impending judgment against the northern kingdom of Israel, driven by moral and social decay. As one delves into the text of Amos, it becomes clear that his pronouncements were primarily against the backdrop of national prosperity tainted by injustice and spiritual complacency. The motif of judgment is clear from the outset: "'I will not revoke the punishment,' says the Lord" (Amos 1:3), a repetitive declaration emphasizing the irrevocable divine decree. This forewarning of judgment is not only a theological assertion but a call to recognize the ethical standards that the people of Israel had transgressed.

One of the key motifs in Amos' message is the "Day of the Lord" (Amos 5:18-20), a term that carried expectations of divine intervention in favor of Israel but was reinterpreted by Amos as a day of darkness and accountability. This significant reversal underscores the prophet's radical challenge to contemporary theological assumptions. Amos presents a stern warning that the covenant relationship with Yahweh demands ethical living and justice, not simply ritualistic observance—a warning encapsulated in his renowned proclamation: "But let justice roll down like waters, and righteousness like an ever-flowing stream" (Amos 5:24).

The themes of justice and righteousness are inextricably linked to Amos' critiques of social inequity. In Amos 2:6-7, the prophet highlights systemic injustices: "They sell the innocent for silver, and the needy for a pair of sandals." The image painted is one of grievous exploitation, where economic greed has superseded human dignity. This thematic concern is a common thread throughout Amos' oracles—

accusations of corruption, exploitation of the poor, and perversion of justice at the city gates (Amos 5:10-12) are indicative of a society in moral disarray. The prophetic call, therefore, is not just to repentance but to transformative action that reinstates social equity.

Furthermore, the theme of accountability extends beyond Israel to neighboring nations (Amos 1:3–2:5), highlighting a universal standard of justice whereby all nations are answerable to God for their transgressions. The broad scope of Amos' condemnation serves to illustrate that the God of Israel is also the God of all creation, enforcing divine justice across geopolitical boundaries.

Additionally, Amos employs vivid imagery and symbolism to communicate his message, from the visions of locusts and plumb lines (Amos 7:1-9) to the profound depiction of a famine "not of bread, nor a thirst for water, but of hearing the words of the Lord" (Amos 8:11). These motifs serve both as illustrative warnings and pedagogical tools, creating a rich tapestry of prophetic literature that compels the audience toward reflection and, ideally, repentance.

In conclusion, the message of judgment in Amos is a tapestry of interwoven themes and motifs designed to awaken a sense of moral urgency and divine accountability. As Amos boldly confronts the complacent and privileged classes, he calls for a return to genuine worship characterized by social justice and righteousness. The enduring relevance of Amos' prophetic vision speaks volumes to the timeless nature of his message and the enduring need for justice within society. Through this exploration of judgment, Amos challenges readers to contemplate their own roles within the divine narrative, urging a life aligned with the principles of justice and faithfulness.

Amos and the Northern Kingdom of Israel

Amos, an eighth-century BCE prophet hailing from the small village of Tekoa, embarked on a pivotal mission to deliver God's message to the Northern Kingdom of Israel. This mission, both geographically and politically challenging, was rooted in divine summons and reflected a complex interplay of sociopolitical factors that characterized the era.

The Northern Kingdom of Israel, with its opulent and fortified cities, starkly contrasted with Amos's humble beginnings as a shepherd and sycamore-fig farmer. During his time, Israel was experiencing a period of prosperity and relative peace under King Jeroboam II. The economic growth and political stability, however, masked underlying issues of social injustice and religious complacency, which Amos was divinely commissioned to address. His mission underscored profound socioeconomic disparities, whereby wealth and power were concentrated in the hands of a few, while the poor and marginalized were oppressed and neglected—a reality Amos vociferously condemned (Amos 2:6-8).

Amos's messages were audacious in their confrontation with the status quo. Unlike prophets aligned with the royal courts, Amos was an outsider with no vested interest in the political structures of the Northern Kingdom. This detachment lent a unique authority to his prophetic voice, allowing him to declare truths without fear or favor. Theological scholar James D. Nogalski elucidates this point, asserting that Amos's independence enabled him to critique systemic injustices with an unyielding devotion to divine will (Nogalski, "The Book of the Twelve," Society of Biblical Literature).

One of the most striking elements of Amos's mission was his unfaltering focus on moral and ethical conduct as a litmus test for true faithfulness to God. In Amos 5:24, he famously implores, "But let justice roll on like a river, righteousness like a never-failing stream!" This prophetic demand encapsulates his vision of a society where divine justice and righteousness transcend empty ritualistic worship, calling for genuine social reform that aligns with covenantal principles.

Amos also faced opposition from established religious and political leaders. The priest Amaziah of Bethel, who served under the auspices of Jeroboam II, viewed Amos's prophecies as threats to the state-endorsed religious institution. In Amos 7:10-17, Amaziah attempts to expel Amos from Israel, accusing him of conspiracy and treason. Amos's response reaffirms his divine commission, unwavering in his claim that his prophetic declarations originate from Yahweh's call, rather than personal ambition.

In delivering his prophetic messages, Amos frequently employs vivid imagery and rhetorical devices. His visions—such as those of locusts, fire, and a plumb line (Amos 7)—serve as symbolic representations of impending divine judgment. Such imagery starkly conveyed the gravity of Israel's moral decline and urgent need for repentance, resonating deeply with a wide audience, capable of understanding these symbols' significance, even if Amos himself faced resistance.

The resonance of Amos's mission to Israel extended beyond his immediate historical context, providing a theological framework that emphasized God's demand for justice and righteousness. His prophetic legacy endures through the ages, inviting ongoing reflection on the social and spiritual dimensions of faith and challenging both ancient and modern audiences to consider the ethical imperatives of divine justice. As Bernard Anderson notes, the essence of Amos's prophecy lies in its timeless demand for moral integrity and alignment with divine purposes (Anderson, "Understanding the Old Testament").

While Amos did not witness the full realization of his prophecies within his lifetime, the destruction of the Northern Kingdom by Assyria in 722 BCE, as forewarned, would echo his somber warnings. His pronouncements, etched into the annals of biblical history, remain a profound testament to the enduring call for justice and faithful obedience to God's will.

The Role of Prophets in Ancient Israel

In the vibrant tapestry of ancient Israel, prophets held a distinctive and pivotal role, representing a bridge between the divine and the mundane. Prophets in this era were not mere conduits of supernatural revelation, but significant arbiters of societal norms, bearers of religious conviction, and moral voices in times of crisis. To fully appreciate the life and mission of Amos, one must delve into the broader spectrum of what prophets symbolized and accomplished in ancient Israel. This exploration not only contextualizes Amos within his historical period but also illuminates the broader prophetic tradition evident throughout the Hebrew Bible.

The Hebrew term for prophet, "navi," stems from a root meaning "to call" or "proclaim." Prophets were individuals called by God to serve as His spokespersons to the people, with messages that often contained both forthright declarations and veiled prophecies. As Merrill F. Unger describes, "a prophet was essentially a human mouthpiece through whom God spoke to humans" (Unger, 1957). This divine call was a foundational attribute, setting prophets apart as uniquely bound to divine will and purpose.

In ancient Israel, the prophets' responsibilities encompassed multiple dimensions. Foremost, they served as intermediaries, conveying God's message to human audiences. Additionally, prophets critiqued and challenged the sociopolitical structures of their time. They often arose in periods of crisis—ethical, military, or spiritual—and delivered admonitions and warnings. Their oracles were not confined to predictions of disaster or hope but encompassed broader theological affirmations regarding the nature of God and His expectations from His chosen people.

Prophets like Amos arose during times of ethical decay, where idolatry, social injustice, and exploitation were rampant. They highlighted the discrepancies between the covenantal ideals and the practices of the Israelite community. "The ethical teachings of the prophets presuppose the existence of a national community living under divine law" (Elmslie, 1915). This assertion underscores the prophets' intrinsic task of recalling the nation to its foundational covenant with Yahweh, to justice, and to the moral law that ought to permeate their societal life.

In Amos's case, his critiques against social injustices were precursors to later social justice movements, highlighting inequalities and exploitation under the guise of religious piety. Amos stood out for his clear messages against the exploitation of the poor and the corrupt practices enshrined by the elite, encapsulated in statements like, "Let justice roll on like a river, righteousness like a never-failing stream!" (Amos

5:24, NIV). This vivid imagery signifies a profound yearning for justice as a continual, unhindered process.

Prophets also fulfilled roles as intercessors, entreating God on behalf of the people. This is particularly evident in instances where impending divine wrath was averted through their supplications. Their intercession was not just a plea for mercy but an effort to realign a wayward nation with its divinely ordained path. An example of this advocacy is seen in Moses, who often pleaded with God to spare Israel from destruction due to their transgressions (Exodus 32:11-14).

In the context of worship and religious practices, prophets frequently critiqued the ritualism that was devoid of true devotion and ethical obedience. They were staunch critics of a religion that prioritized ceremonies over sincere worship and righteous living. This critical stance is famously voiced in Amos's oracles (Amos 5:21-23), where he declares God's disdain for feasts and assemblies unsupported by genuine ethical behavior.

The role of prophets in ancient Israel, therefore, transcended mere predictions. It was a multi-faceted ministry deeply embedded within the fabric of societal norms, aligning them closer to divine expectations. Amos, along with his prophetic contemporaries, exemplified these roles, leaving indelible marks that reverberated through subsequent religious thought and interpretation. This profound legacy speaks not only to their historical and theological importance but also to the timeless messages they conveyed which continue to resonate with contemporary audiences seeking to balance spirituality with social conscience.

The enduring legacy of prophets illuminates the vital responsivity they embraced: echoing as commentators on the moral and ethical dimensions of society. Their voices, though situated in antiquity, traverse time to challenge each generation anew, urging adherence to a justice that aligns with divine righteousness. To truly grasp their enduring influence, one must not only read their words but internalize the deep moral and theological discourse they initiate—a dialogue with the divine that compels a response from humankind.

Amos' Visions and Prophetic Symbolism

Amos, an 8th-century BCE prophet originally from Tekoa, a small town in Judah, stands as one of the most provocative figures in the biblical text. His prophetic ministry, primarily directed towards the Northern Kingdom of Israel, is marked by vivid imagery and compelling visions. Amos' visions serve not only as vehicles for divine communication but also as profound symbolic representations that convey deep theological truths.

The visions of Amos are integral to his prophetic message and reveal essential aspects of God's character and the conditions of Israel. The prophetic symbolism within these visions encapsulates divine judgment, social critique, and moral expectation, reflecting Amos' role as a harbinger of divine retribution.

One of the significant visions bestowed upon Amos is the vision of the locusts (Amos 7:1-3). This vision, characterized by its stark and disturbing imagery, portrays a swarm of locusts consuming the land after the king's mowings. The locusts represent an impending calamity, symbolizing God's judgment due to Israel's persistent sinfulness and societal injustice. However, the vision also highlights intercessory potential; Amos pleads with God, and God relents, demonstrating His mercy.

Moreover, the vision of the devouring fire (Amos 7:4-6) follows, where a great fire consumes the deep and devours the land. This vision symbolizes the all-encompassing nature of God's judgment, suggesting an inevitable destruction due to Israel's moral decay. Yet, once again, Amos' intercession results in divine concession, underscoring a balance between justice and compassion.

The subsequent vision of the plumb line (Amos 7:7-9) introduces a different dimension of symbolic representation. The plumb line signifies a standard of righteousness against which the people of Israel are measured. Unlike the earlier visions, there is no intercession in this scenario, highlighting the inevitability of judgment as Israel has failed to meet God's righteous standards. This vision powerfully communicates God's commitment to justice and the consequence of societal inequity.

Another compelling vision is the basket of summer fruit (Amos 8:1-3), symbolizing the ripeness of Israel for judgment. The imagery conveys the urgency and certainty of the impending divine judgment. The Hebrew wordplay between "summer fruit" (qayits) and "end" (qets) conveys a prophetic announcement—Israel's societal and moral corruption has reached its climax, warranting comprehensive judgment.

Lastly, the vision of the Lord standing beside the altar (Amos 9:1) portrays a more direct divine intervention. The destruction of the temple and the call for judgment illustrates the termination of a current religious order corrupted by injustice and insincerity. It is here that Amos signals an eschatological hope—the promise of restoration and the reestablishment of the Davidic line, indicating divine mercy's ultimate triumph.

Amos' visions are rich in symbolic imagery and serve to communicate profound theological insights concerning God's nature, the necessity of justice, and the consequences of societal decay. These symbols transcend the specifics of their historical context, offering timeless principles applicable to any context where justice and righteousness are in jeopardy. The visionary experiences of Amos remind readers that divine communication often comprises symbolic, intense, and sometimes dramatic imagery to convey subjective truths with objective clarity.

The engagement with the prophetic symbolism of Amos thus necessitates thoughtful reflection and discernment, encouraging readers to consider the symbolic messages in the broader narrative of God and humanity. As such, Amos' visions solidify his legacy as a prophet who challenges complacency and invites his audience into a profound encounter with the divine.

Contrasts with Contemporary Prophets

Amid the backdrop of the 8th century BCE, the voice of Amos arises distinct and commanding, echoing through the socio-political corridors of ancient Israel. A study of Amos, when juxtaposed against his prophetic contemporaries, unveils a tapestry rich with contrasts and nuances that are as illuminating as they are profound. This exploration into the differences between Amos and other prophetic figures of his time, such as Hosea, Isaiah, and Micah, provides a deeper understanding of his unique role and mission in the landscape of biblical prophecy.

Amos, a herdsman and sycamore fig grower from the small village of Tekoa, epitomizes the archetype of an outsider, both geographically and socially, when considered against prophets like Isaiah, who was closely connected with the royal court in Jerusalem. This distinction is crucial in comprehending the genesis of Amos' prophetic messages. Unlike Isaiah, whose insights into divine mandates often intertwined with royal politics, Amos' origin from Judah but mission to the Northern Kingdom of Israel underscores a voice untainted by political alliances or courtly influences.

In contrast, Hosea, another notable prophet contemporaneous with Amos, shared the common mission territory of the Northern Kingdom. However, their approaches were markedly different. While Hosea's prophecies often utilized the metaphor of marital fidelity to symbolize the covenantal relationship between God and Israel—a motif rich with emotional and relational depth—Amos employed stark and vivid imagery of social and economic justice. His denunciation of superficial religiosity amidst systemic injustice (Amos 5:21-24) deviated sharply from Hosea's concentration on idolatry and faithfulness, suggesting a uniquely socio-economic and ethical framework within which Amos operated.

The prophetic methodology of Amos also diverges significantly from that of Micah. Both prophets decried social injustices, yet Amos' declarations are primarily directed at Israel's higher echelons of power and wealth, articulating a vehement critique of societal inequity and corruption. Micah, while sharing this concern for social justice, extended it with profound rural overtones, reflecting the plight of peasantries under oppressive city dwellers. Amos, in his urban-focused critique, reveals an acute awareness of the complexities faced within burgeoning city centers in Israel, exhibiting a sophisticated socio-religious rhetoric targeting those who manipulate power.

The thematic core of Amos' prophecies—the vehement call for justice and righteousness—serves as a critical hallmark distinguishing him from his contemporaries. Whereas other prophets occasionally blended comforting narratives within their messages of admonition (for instance, Isaiah's prophecies of a future hope), Amos remains steadfast in his harsh rhetoric without inserting significant elements of consolation or hope until the book's final oracle (Amos 9:11-15), and even this is debated by scholars as possibly being a later addition.

Furthermore, the portrayal of Amos in these dire messages reflects a particular theological conviction pertaining to divine justice. While many prophets emphasize the covenantal relationship and Israel's breaches thereof, Amos articulated a version of divine justice that is unyielding and cosmic. His view on the Day of the Lord, for example, is sobering and counter to the hopeful anticipation found in the utterances of others, painting it instead as a day of darkness (Amos 5:18-20), reinforcing his untarnished picture of God as the sovereign arbiter of justice.

The contrasts between Amos and his contemporaries culminate in a nuanced understanding of his mission. As scholars like J. Barton have noted, the distinction lies not within an absence of shared themes with other prophets, but in the unwavering and unembellished manner in which Amos conveyed God's judgement. His theological insights eschewed allegorical softness in favor of direct, unmitigated declarations that pressed the Northern Kingdom to a point of unavoidable reflection and, albeit unheeded, repentance.

In summation, Amos, within the gallery of his contemporary prophets, stands out as a singularly profound voice against injustice, unimpeded by personal, social, or political encumbrances. His prophetic artistry, grounded in his own unique experiences and perceptions of divine will, constructed a narrative that not only spoke to his time with unmatched clarity but also reverberated through the corridors of history to infuse subsequent discourses on morality and righteousness. Ultimately, his distinct contrasts with contemporary prophets continue to offer a rich lens through which modern readers can explore the complex dynamics of biblical prophecy.

The Legacy and Influence of Amos' Prophecy

The Book of Amos stands as a seminal piece of prophetic literature, offering insights not only into the sociopolitical climate of ancient Israel but also into the enduring nature of prophetic discourse. The legacy of Amos' prophecy is profound, impacting both contemporaneous society and subsequent theological thought.

Amos' arrival on the prophetic scene as a figure from Tekoa offered a unique voice—one from outside the traditional prophetic cadre. His background as a herdsman and grower of sycamore figs (Amos 7:14) provided him with a perspective rooted in everyday realities, allowing him to speak with an authenticity and authority that resonated within the societal structures of Israel. His unyielding emphasis on justice and righteousness (Amos 5:24) served as a sharp critique of the systemic inequities prevalent in the Northern Kingdom, marking a pivotal moment in the prophetic tradition.

The influence of Amos' prophecy extended beyond his immediate historical context. His messages of judgment and divine justice were precursors that influenced future prophetic voices. The call for social justice, punctuated by vivid imagery and symbolic visions, set a standard for prophetic engagement with social issues—standards that would echo through the messages of Isaiah, Jeremiah, and the so-called "Minor Prophets."

Furthermore, Amos' legacy is seen in the development of eschatological themes in later biblical texts. His dire warnings of judgment—and yet, subtle undertones of hope and restoration—can be traced in the eschatological visions found in books like Daniel and Revelation. His prophecy essentially sketched the contours of divine intervention, showing not only what happens when justice is perverted but also the potential for renewal, an idea captured succinctly in God's promise of restoration (Amos 9:11-15).

To understand Amos' influence, one must consider his innovative use of language and imagery. As the scholar James Limburg notes, Amos employed a range of rhetorical devices—such as litanies of woes, rhetorical questions, and stark parallelisms—that both captivated and chastised his audience (Limburg, 1987). His language crafted a narrative that was not only memorable but also deeply dissociative from the false assurances offered by other contemporary figures (Amos 8:11-12).

Beyond the biblical canon, Amos' prophecies have left indelible marks on theological and ethical thought throughout the ages. His advocacy for justice has resonated throughout church history; notably, during periods such as the Reformation and the Civil Rights Movement. His concerns echo in the sermons of Martin Luther King Jr., who appealed to Amos' call for "justice to roll down like waters" as a clarion call for civil rights (King, 1963).

In academic circles, the Book of Amos continues to fuel scholarly dialogue regarding the nature and purpose of prophecy. His straightforward declaration that he was neither a prophet by trade nor the son of a prophet (Amos 7:14)—but rather called by God—serves as a crucial case study in understanding the dynamics of divine calling and human agency. Theological discourse continues to grapple with Amos' legacy, especially with respect to how one can discern authentic prophetic voices in contemporary contexts.

In essence, Amos' prophecies underscore a perennial truth: that divine justice demands unwavering adherence to moral and ethical norms, with an urgency that transcends ages. His influence, thus, is not solely academic or religious but also profoundly practical, challenging each generation to evaluate its own adherence to the tenets of justice and righteousness.

In conclusion, the legacy and influence of Amos are multi-faceted, spanning immediate historical implications, theological developments across centuries, and ongoing ethical discourses. Amos challenges readers to heed the call to justice with a sincerity and urgency that remains as relevant today as it was in the eighth century BCE. The potency of his prophecy, rooted in a profound understanding of divine justice, continues to inspire and provoke action toward a more equitable world.

References:

Limburg, James. *Encountering the Book of Amos: A Commentary.* Westminster John Knox Press, 1987.

King, Martin Luther Jr. "I Have a Dream." Delivered at the Lincoln Memorial, Washington, D.C., August 28, 1963.

Themes and Messages in the Book of Amos

Divine Justice and Righteousness

The book of Amos, a cornerstone of Old Testament theology, offers a profound exploration of divine justice and righteousness, woven intricately into the fabric of its prophetic messages. As one delves into the themes presented by Amos, it becomes evident that divine justice is not merely a distant ideal but a tangible demand placed upon the people of Israel, reflecting God's inherent nature and expectations for human conduct.

Amos's depiction of divine justice is deeply rooted in the character of God as presented throughout the Hebrew Scriptures. The prophet Amos fervently emphasizes that the Lord is not only a deity of covenant but also one who acts with unwavering righteousness and will not tolerate injustice, irrespective of its source. This principle is clearly encapsulated in Amos 5:24, "But let justice roll on like a river, righteousness like a never-failing stream." Here, the imagery of an ever-flowing stream powerfully conveys the perpetual and inevitable nature of divine justice, demanding consistent moral and ethical behavior from the people. This is indicative of a divine mandate to uphold justice irrespective of societal norms or personal convenience.

Amos persistently highlights that divine justice is intricately linked with righteousness, where the two are inseparable and mutually inclusive. In the biblical context, righteousness (Hebrew: צֶדֶק, tzedek) is not simply about personal morality but encompasses social relationships and communal well-being. Amos's message resonates with the notions found in other prophetic writings, such as in Isaiah and Hosea, which assert God's concerns not only for religious formalism but also for ethical living and social responsibility. Thus, Amos propels his audience towards a holistic understanding of worship, which integrates spiritual faithfulness with authentic lifestyle practices characterized by justice and care for the marginalized.

This prophetic framework challenges the prevailing perception during Amos's time that religious rituals alone were sufficient for maintaining a relationship with God. Instead, Amos emphatically denounces superficial religiosity that neglects righteousness and perpetuates social inequity. This denunciation is notably evident in Amos 5:21-23, where the prophet proclaims God's disdain for their feasts and offerings which fail to embody justice and righteousness. Amos thus redirects the Israelites' focus from outward observance to inner transformation, urging them to seek justice as a true expression of divine worship.

Amos's discourse on divine justice also serves as an ethical imperative; it requires active participation in societal reform. The prophet calls for repentance that transcends individual piety and engenders community-wide renewal. He advocates for the reestablishment of social systems that are equitable and just, wherein all individuals are valued and cared for in accordance with God's righteous standards. The consistent message of Amos is that divine justice is a communal mandate, requiring systemic change that is grounded in love, mercy, and truth.

A remarkable aspect of Amos's prophecy is its timeless relevance. The themes of divine justice and righteousness transcend their historical context and echo throughout the centuries, resonating with contemporary issues of social justice, equality, and human rights. The call for justice as a flowing river challenges modern audiences to reflect on their societal structures and personal roles in perpetuating or combating systemic injustices. Amos's vision prompts an evaluation of moral integrity and the pursuit of a just society in alignment with divine principles.

The integration of justice and righteousness in Amos moves beyond mere theological constructs; it serves as a practical guide for living out faith authentically in all realms of life. By internalizing this prophetic vision, individuals and communities today can strive towards a model of faithfulness that mirrors the divine nature of God — characterized by love, justice, and righteousness — thereby fulfilling Amos's enduring call to justice that flows eternally. This legacy of Amos not only challenges but inspires believers to embody divine principles, fostering societies that stand as testimonies to the righteous character of the living God.

Social Injustice and Oppression

In the profound tapestry of prophetic literature, the Book of Amos stands as a clarion call against systemic social injustice and oppression. As we delve into the themes of social injustice and oppression within the Book of Amos, it becomes apparent that the prophet's message is as much about societal equity as it is about spiritual fidelity. The prophet Amos, though hailing from the rural town of Tekoa, addressed the urban society of Israel with an unyielding critique of their social inequities.

Amos's message was delivered during a time of economic prosperity in the Northern Kingdom of Israel under King Jeroboam II. This wealth, however, was unequally distributed; the elite lived in opulence while the poor languished in poverty, a disparity that Amos decried fervently. His prophetic proclamations underscore the plight of the marginalized and the grave failures of the ruling class who perpetuated systems of inequality. As Martin Luther King Jr. once alluded to the enduring relevance of social justice when he noted, "Injustice anywhere is a threat to justice everywhere" (King, 1963), so too did Amos resonate with this timeless truth.

The motifs of social injustice and oppression manifest vividly throughout Amos's oracles. In Amos 2:6-7, the Lord condemns Israel for "selling the righteous for silver, and the needy for a pair of sandals." These words illustrate the commodification of humanity, where basic human dignity is traded for material gain. The elite's exploitation of the poor highlighted profound moral failings, illustrating a society where economic transactions trumped ethical considerations. Furthermore, the debasement of justice is poignantly captured in Amos 5:12, where the prophet declares, "For I know how many are your transgressions and how great are your sins—you who afflict the righteous, who take a bribe, and turn aside the needy in the gate."

Such passages reveal that in Amos's time, even judicial systems, ostensibly designed to protect the innocent and uphold fairness, were corrupted by greed and malfeasance. The city gate, traditionally a place of justice, had become a venue for injustice, where bribery dictated verdicts and the vulnerable were denied justice. The prophet's audacity to denounce these ills resonates within the framework of ethical monotheism, insisting on the inseparability of justice and worship.

Amos's condemnation is not merely aimed at those who commit overt acts of injustice, but also at those who are complicit through their indifference and passivity. As Abraham Joshua Heschel expounded, "An act remains a major disaster" if humanity silently ignores it (Heschel, 1962). Amos admonishes not only the perpetrators but also those who stand idly by in the face of such systemic wrongs. His writings present a call to active engagement in rectifying social ills.

The nexus between social stability and moral accountability is emphasized throughout the narrative. Amos 6:4-6 castigates those who are "at ease in Zion," reveling in their luxury while oblivious to the "collapse of Joseph," a metaphor for societal decay. The imagery of banquets, fine oils, and musical soirees starkly contrasts with the silence towards societal injustice, serving as a potent reminder that true peace and prosperity cannot coexist with systemic oppression.

Importantly, the social critique within Amos extends beyond mere condemnation. It carries within it the seeds of restoration and hope, advocating for a return to covenantal faithfulness, where justice "rolls on like a river, righteousness like a never-failing stream!" (Amos 5:24). This vision of divine justice presupposes an active role of individuals to engage in moral rectitude, remove structural inequities, and uphold the dignity of every human being.

In analyzing the rich narrative of social justice within Amos, modern readers are compelled to reflect on contemporary societal structures. Are the issues of oppression, economic disparity, and judicial imbalance not echoed in today's world? As biblical scholarship continues to unravel the layers of Amos's message, it remains evident that the prophet's call for justice presents both a profound theological discourse and a practical ethic. The Book of Amos challenges its audience, both ancient and modern, to transcend a mere spiritual confession and engage robustly in the pursuit of justice and equity, affirming that faithfulness to God is inextricably linked to the way we treat our fellow human beings.

The exploration of social injustice within the Book of Amos provides a paradigmatic lens through which the interconnectedness of societal welfare and covenantal fidelity is viewed. It is a timeless appeal to each generation to right the wrongs of society through active and meaningful participation in justice, reminding us that true worship of the Divine can never be divorced from our ethical responsibilities in the world. In so doing, Amos profoundly integrates the spiritual and social dimensions, inviting a holistic approach towards understanding righteousness and justice as divinely ordained imperatives.

The Day of the Lord

The concept of the "Day of the Lord" is a pivotal theme in the Book of Amos, as it encapsulates both divine judgment and eschatological hope, intertwining historical realities with future expectations. The prophetic literature often presents this day as an anticipated occasion when God will enact justice and bring about renewal. In understanding this multi-faceted concept, we must delve into both the immediate historical implications for the ancient Israelites and its broader theological significance within the biblical narrative.

Amos, one of the earliest writing prophets, delivered his message during a time of relative peace and prosperity in the Northern Kingdom of Israel. Yet, beneath this façade of stability lay rampant corruption, social injustice, and spiritual complacency. The "Day of the Lord," as articulated by Amos, serves as a divine response to these conditions. Amos 5:18-20 warns, "Woe to you who desire the day of the Lord! Why would you have the day of the Lord? It is darkness, and not light."

This passage starkly contrasts with the popular perception among the Israelites, who viewed the "Day of the Lord" as a time when God would vindicate them against their enemies. Amos subverts this expectation by proclaiming that this day would not bring deliverance, but rather judgment. It underscores a profound irony: God's people, expecting salvation, would instead face the very wrath they wished upon their foes, highlighting that divine justice is not bound by nationalistic or ethnocentric biases.

The "Day of the Lord" in Amos serves a dual purpose. First, it acts as a climactic warning against hypocrisy and moral corruption. The notion that God would punish His own people as He would any other nation was a radical idea, challenging the complacency borne out of Israel's covenantal status. This perspective reinforces the book's overarching theme that righteousness and justice are core tenets of a life pleasing to God. Allegiance to God demands ethical living, as seen in Amos 5:24: "But let justice roll down like waters, and righteousness like an ever-flowing stream."

Secondly, the "Day of the Lord" serves as an instrument of ultimate hope and restoration. Through the cataclysm of judgment, there lies a promise of eventual restoration and renewal. Amos 9:11-15 speaks of rebuilding the fallen tent of David and restoring the fortunes of His people, re-establishing a remnant that will seek God's true worship and justice. This eschatological promise represents the consummation of divine justice where, despite impending doom, hope persists for those who repent and turn back to the path of righteousness.

The theological implications of this theme permeate both contemporary and later biblical thought. It sets a precedent for subsequent prophetic literature and New Testament eschatology, where the "Day of the Lord" is not confined to a specific time and place but is an enduring moral imperative. It calls for vigilance in maintaining justice and righteousness while offering hope for divine intervention in rectifying the world's wrongs.

Therefore, the "Day of the Lord" in Amos is a profoundly sobering concept. It reveals the vanguard of divine justice and grace: a cautionary pronouncement for complacent society and an aspirational vision for the future. In turn, this demands that readers and believers remain engaged in a continuous moral assessment, aligning themselves with the divine ideals of justice emblazoned within the prophetic words of Amos.

This duality of judgment and promise compels us to reckon with our own contexts, urging us to reflect on how righteousness and justice manifest in our society, inspired by the ancient cry of the prophet whose words ring as true today as they did centuries ago. The "Day of the Lord" remains a powerful reminder that God's justice is omnipresent and His mercy ever-available for those who seek transformation.

Israel's Covenant and Responsibility

The Book of Amos stands out as a profound narrative on the covenantal obligations of Israel, articulated with passion and urgency by the prophet Amos. At its core, this narrative asserts the unbreakable bonds of accountability tied to the covenant between Yahweh and Israel, a covenant whose terms and implications are vividly expressed throughout the scriptural discourse.

Amos, believed to have prophesied in the 8th century BCE during the reigns of Uzziah in Judah and Jeroboam II in Israel, operates within a socio-political and religious framework where the Northern Kingdom of Israel stood in glaring defiance of the original Yahwistic covenant. The historical landscape at this time was one of economic prosperity for Israel, often leading to social stratification and moral decay, a backdrop against which Amos's messages are stark reminders of divine expectations as outlined in the covenant.

Central to Israel's covenantal responsibility in Amos's proclamation is a call for justice and righteousness. The Hebrew Bible consistently presents the covenant not merely as a set of laws but as a relationship requiring justice toward fellow humans as an expression of faithfulness to God. Amos 5:24 encapsulates this principle succinctly: "But let justice roll on like a river, righteousness like a never-failing stream!" This call to uphold justice is situated in a covenantal context implying that neglecting social justice is not just a societal issue but a breach of the divine agreement with Yahweh.

Furthermore, the covenant demands true worship and genuine devotion, free from hypocrisy and empty ritualism. Amos's critique of Israel's worship is that it had become disconnected from ethical living. Worship had become an 'abomination' when divorced from the moral and ethical behavior expected by the covenant. The prophet denounces the festivals and sacrifices in Amos 5:21-23, stating, "I hate, I despise your religious festivals; your assemblies are a stench to me...away with the noise of your songs!" This condemnation highlights that adherence to the covenant was not just about ritual adherence but involved living a life that mirrors God's justice and righteousness.

Israel's covenant responsibility extends into the realm of societal relationships. The covenant implores the nation to reflect God's holy character in its dealings by upholding the dignity and welfare of all, especially the vulnerable. Amos charges Israel with neglecting the poor and perverting justice for the sake of gain, actions that starkly contravene the covenant laws laid down in the Torah, particularly those in Deuteronomy that call for the protection and fair treatment of the widow, the orphan, and the alien.

Amos unrelentingly reminds Israel that its privileged status as a chosen nation brings with it demands for higher standards of behavior. In Amos 3:2, God declares, "You only have I chosen of all the families of the earth; therefore I will punish you for all your sins." This statement underscores the principle that covenant intimacy entails accountability. Israel's failure to live up to the divine standards leads to discussions of impending judgment, yet even within these pronouncements lies an implicit call to repentance, an opportunity to return to Yahweh's ways and thus fulfill their covenant duties.

The prophetic literature of Amos serves not only as a historical diagnostic of Israel's failings but also as a powerful instructional template for understanding God's endless pursuit of social justice aligned with covenantal fidelity. For those studying and interpreting the Book of Amos, engaging with

Israel's covenantal responsibilities reveals profound insights into both historical obligations and timeless moral imperatives.

Visions of Judgment

The Book of Amos, an integral component of the Minor Prophets in the Old Testament, is a rich tapestry of divine visions and declarations. Among these, the visions of judgment stand out profoundly, encapsulating the dire warnings and imminent consequences of the transgressions committed by the people of Israel. These visions offer a vivid portrayal of the divine perspective and serve as a call to heed and rectify the erroneous paths embarked upon by the society of that time.

Amos, a shepherd and dresser of sycamore figs from Tekoa, was tasked by Yahweh to deliver a message that was not only a direct reflection of divine discontent but also a roadmap of impending judgment. The subtext of this divine communication through visions underscores the prophetic literature's complexity and the necessity for a nuanced understanding of its messages.

The visions, as recorded in the Book of Amos, primarily occur in chapters seven through nine and can be segmented into distinct portrayals, each carrying a specific indictment and subsequent consequence. One of the most notable is the vision of the locust swarm (Amos 7:1-3). Here, Amos envisions a devastating plague of locusts symbolizing the incursion and subsequent consumption of the land's prosperity. This plague is illustrative of the impending socio-economic and spiritual desolation due to Israel's failure to live up to the covenantal expectations. Reflecting on this vision, scholar Jörg Jeremias asserts, "The vision of the locusts serves as a warning against the complacent attitude of those who assume immunity from divine consequences."

This is soon followed by the vision of the devouring fire (Amos 7:4-6), which signifies an even more profound calamity—a consuming judgment scorches not only the terrestrial realm but seeks to penetrate the very heart of the nation's consciousness. The imagery of fire here transcends mere physical destruction; it alludes to the extinction of Israel's moral and ethical fabric. Terrence E. Fretheim comments that this vision "compels readers to reconsider their perceptions of safety and provoke a transformation in understanding the gravity of divine expectations."

The narrative escalates with the vision of the plumb line (Amos 7:7-9), wherein God is depicted as a carpenter measuring the integrity of Israel with a plumb line. This imagery poignantly signifies God's precise and unyielding standards, revealing the inherent flaws and the inability of Israel to maintain the moral and spiritual rectitude required. This vision diverges from mere earthly judgments and shifts the conversation towards spiritual integrity and its absence in society. As noted by Walter Brueggemann, "The plumb line vision insists on the notion of unavoidable accountability and the moral geometry of divine justice."

The next vision, that of summer fruit (Amos 8:1-3), communicates a sense of impending demise—Israel has reached the zenith of its rebellion, akin to ripe fruit ready to spoil. Amos links this imagery to the Hebrew word for "end" (qayits), signifying that the end is nigh for Israel due to its persistent inequities and inattention to divine mandates. This particular vision points to the thematic culmination of divine patience, warning that the societal and spiritual decay will lead to its unavoidable end. James L. Mays interprets this as a demonstration of a "moment of grace before inescapable verdict," indicative of an opportunity squandered.

Finally, the series of visions culminates in the vision of the Lord beside the altar (Amos 9:1-4), marking the climax of divine judgment. This vision shifts scenes to the sanctuary, which is intended as a refuge and place of divine encounter. Here, however, it becomes a site of judgment and condemnation, indicating that no aspect of life is immune to divine scrutiny. As Carol J. Dempsey has observed, "The universal scope of this final vision mirrors the penetrating gaze of the divine that sees beyond mere ritual to the heart of human fidelity."

These visionary passages within the Book of Amos serve as profound theological and moral reflections pertinent to the contemporary reader. They reveal not only the divine response to societal corruption and spiritual negligence but also provide insight into the nature of divine justice and the imperative for societal transformation. For those examining biblical narratives with a theological lens, the visions of judgment in Amos invite a deeper exploration of the conversation between the divine and humanity, a dialogue marked by the severity of judgment intertwined with the persistent hope for redemption. The visions evoke a profound sense of urgency, compelling individuals and communities alike to heed the potent mix of divine decree against injustice and the hope for a repentant return to covenantal faithfulness. As we navigate modern societal complexities, the visionary insights from Amos underscore that the past remains a powerfully resonant voice in the quest for justice and righteousness today.

The Prophet's Role and Mission

The Book of Amos, situated among the Minor Prophets in the Old Testament, offers a profound insight into the role and mission of the prophet amidst the socio-political and religious landscape of 8th century BCE Israel. Understanding Amos's mission is critical to interpreting his messages, as his role was not merely to foretell events but to act as a conduit for divine admonition and guidance.

Amos, originally from the southern kingdom of Judah, was called by God to prophesy in the northern kingdom of Israel during a period of relative prosperity and peace under King Jeroboam II. As documented in Amos 7:14-15, Amos declared, "I was neither a prophet nor the son of a prophet, but I was a shepherd, and I also took care of sycamore-fig trees. But the Lord took me from tending the flock and said to me, 'Go, prophesy to my people Israel'" (NIV). His humble origins underscore that true prophetic calling does not arise from social status, but divine election.

Amos's role encompassed several dimensions. Primarily, he served as the mouthpiece of Yahweh, delivering messages that emphasized divine justice and righteousness. Unlike the professional prophets of his time, whose positions were often tied to the royal court or cultic enterprises, Amos stood apart, unencumbered by political allegiances or economic incentives. His mission was thus characterized by a fervent commitment to truth, disrupting complacency in matters of morality and worship.

The heart of Amos's mission was to call Israel to account for its covenantal failures. The Israelites had entered into a covenant relationship with God, which demanded adherence to standards of justice and communal responsibility (Amos 3:1-2). Therefore, the prophet's role was akin to that of a prosecuting attorney in a divine court, bringing charges against the nation for transgressions such as idolatry, social inequity, and religious hypocrisy. This prophetic function is encapsulated in Amos's declarations found in Amos 5:24, where he famously exhorts, "But let justice roll on like a river, righteousness like a never-failing stream" (NIV).

Furthermore, Amos's mission involved delivering messages that were not only corrective but also eschatological and hopeful in nature. Despite his harsh pronouncements of judgment, Amos conveyed the possibility of restoration and renewal. His prophecies concluded with a promise of future restoration for the remnant of Jacob (Amos 9:11-15), providing a theological framework for understanding the balance of divine justice and mercy.

Amos's role extended beyond the immediacy of his prophetic address, reaching future generations with enduring teachings on social justice. His mission was an anticipatory guide for readers, encouraging reflection on moral, ethical, and spiritual issues within their own societal contexts. As scholars like Shalom Paul (1991) highlight, "Amos confronts us with divine ethical demands that refuse to be mitigated or compromised."

The crucial component of Amos's mission was his confrontational approach towards the establishment. He was relentless in addressing the leaders and citizens of Israel, unmasking their religious pretenses and exposing their societal flaws. This unwavering commitment reflects a prophetic tradition that considered moral and ethical righteousness non-negotiable divine expectations.

Moreover, Amos's prophetic methodology was profoundly pedagogical. Through rhetorical devices such as rhetorical questions, irony, and vivid imagery, Amos engaged his audience's intellect and emotions, fostering a reflective and transformative listening experience. His ability to weave social critique with theological discourse exemplifies the quintessential characteristics of prophetic literature.

In sum, the role and mission of the prophet Amos were multidimensional and transformative. As God's envoy, Amos articulated a radical vision for a just society grounded in covenantal fidelity. While his messages addressed the immediate crises of his time, they transcended historical boundaries, challenging readers across generations to reevaluate their own commitments to divine justice and ethical living. As we delve deeper into the Book of Amos, it becomes evident that his prophetic voice forms a cornerstone in the ongoing discourse of moral accountability and religious sincerity. Such enduring relevance highlights Amos's pivotal role not only as an ancient Israelite prophet but as a timeless advocate for justice and righteousness.

The Call to Repentance

In the Book of Amos, the call to repentance stands as a clarion declaration amidst a cacophony of judgment and warnings. This call is a profound appeal for transformation, woven into the divine discourse delivered by the prophet Amos. As a native of Tekoa, Amos was summoned by God to prophesy during a time of significant social and religious disarray in the Northern Kingdom of Israel (Wolff, 1977). His prophecies, characterized by astute social criticism and theological reflections, underscore the necessity of repentance as a means of averting impending divine judgment.

The concept of repentance, derived from the Hebrew term *"shuv,"* implies a turning back or reversal of direction (Brueggemann, 2003). It is not merely an acknowledgment of wrongdoing but a conscious decision to return to the covenantal obligations established between Israel and Yahweh. Amos's indictment of Israelite society is clear: their prosperity and religious activities are futile if not accompanied by genuine moral and ethical reforms. As written in Amos 5:14-15, "Seek good and not evil, that you may live; and so the Lord, the God of hosts, will be with you, as you have said. Hate evil and love good, and establish justice in the gate; it may be that the Lord, the God of hosts, will be gracious to the remnant of Joseph" (English Standard Version). This passage encapsulates the essence of Amos's message by coupling divine favor with ethical transformation.

Amos's clarion call to repentance is rooted in the universal principles of divine justice and righteousness. While earlier chapters explore this theme distinctively, it finds nuanced expression within the call to change of heart. God's justice is inextricably linked with Israel's adherence to ethical norms, fostering a societal framework where the weak are protected, and the afflicted are given justice (Paul, 1991). Amos unambiguously critiques a superficial religiosity that substitutes genuine worship with ritualistic practices devoid of moral intent. This critique is particularly evident in Amos 5:21-24, where God expresses disdain for the people's offerings and assemblies because they lack righteousness and justice: "But let justice roll down like waters, and righteousness like an ever-flowing stream."

The socio-economic critique present in Amos's prophecies is expounded upon in another section of this chapter but serves as a pertinent context for the call to repentance. The prophet's lament against economic disparities and systemic oppression spotlights the moral failings undergirding these societal structures. Thus, the call to repentance necessitates a collective realignment towards just economic practices and the equitable distribution of resources.

It is critical to acknowledge the role of covenant theology in Amos's call to repentance. Israel's historical covenant with Yahweh demanded not only religious fidelity but also compliance with ethical imperatives. The prophet reminds his audience of their covenantal responsibilities, urging them to return to a God who desires not sacrifice, but a transformed heart and society.

From a literary standpoint, Amos employs vivid imagery and rhetorical devices to engage his audience in his message. The use of rhetorical questions, lamentation, and direct divine speech styles enhances the urgency and emotive appeal in the call to repentance. Such literary techniques ensure that the message penetrates deeply, calling for an introspective examination among its hearers (Mays, 1969).

In conclusion, the call to repentance in the Book of Amos is a dynamic and multifaceted appeal. It challenges contemporary readers to reflect personally and communally, urging a return to principles of justice and relational fidelity with the divine. This message, when understood within its broader theological context, continues to resonate as a powerful prompt for ethical and spiritual transformation (Gowan, 1988).

References:
- Brueggemann, W. (2003). *An Introduction to the Old Testament: The Canon and Christian Imagination*. Westminster John Knox Press.
- Gowan, D. (1988). *Theology of the Prophetic Books: The Death and Resurrection of Israel*. Westminster John Knox Press.
- Mays, J.L. (1969). *Amos: A Commentary*. SCM Press Ltd.
- Paul, S.M. (1991). *Amos: A Commentary on the Book of Amos*. Hermeneia—a Critical and Historical Commentary on the Bible.
- Wolff, H.W. (1977). *Joel and Amos: A Commentary on the Books of the Prophets Joel and Amos*. Fortress Press.

Economic Inequality Critique

The Book of Amos presents a profound critique of economic inequality, a theme that resonates across the centuries and holds striking relevance in today's global context. Amos, a shepherd from Tekoa, emerges as a voice of moral clarity and divine instruction, decrying the glaring economic disparities of his time. These disparities were not merely socioeconomic concerns; they reflected a deeper, systemic injustice linked intricately to the spiritual apathy and moral failings of Israel. In assessing the economic inequality critique in the Book of Amos, we delve into how this ancient text navigates the intersection of wealth, power, and divine mandate, asserting a call for justice and righteousness.

Amos appears at a time of relative prosperity in the Northern Kingdom of Israel, during the reign of Jeroboam II (circa 786–746 BCE). This period, although characterized by economic affluence, was also marked by significant social stratification. The prophetic text opens a window into a society where economic prosperity is enjoyed by a few at the expense of the many, with wealth accumulation leading to increased social injustice. Amos 6:4-6 vividly portrays the opulence of the elite: "You lie on beds adorned with ivory and lounge on your couches. You dine on choice lambs and fattened calves. You strum away on your harps like David and improvise on musical instruments. You drink wine by the bowlful and use the finest lotions, but you do not grieve over the ruin of Joseph" (NIV). The imagery here is stark, underscoring the moral blindness of the ruling classes who indulge in luxury while ignoring the plight of the marginalized.

The socio-economic critique in Amos largely centers on the exploitation of the poor by the affluent. Amos 2:6-7 (NIV) articulates this injustice: "They sell the innocent for silver, and the needy for a pair of sandals. They trample on the heads of the poor as on the dust of the ground and deny justice to the oppressed." This severe indictment highlights a reprehensible commodification of human life itself, where economic transactions overshadow moral responsibilities. Such economic practices were not only ethically abhorrent but were seen as egregious breaches of the covenantal laws that emphasized justice, mercy, and the protection of the vulnerable (Deuteronomy 15:7-11).

Furthermore, Amos critiques not only the economic oppressors but also the judicial systems that enable and perpetuate such inequalities. The prophet castigates the systemic corruption present in the legal institutions, as indicated in Amos 5:10-13 (NIV): "There are those who hate the one who upholds justice in court and detest the one who tells the truth...Therefore the prudent keep quiet in such times, for the times are evil." This points to a society wherein truth and justice are compromised by the vested interests of the powerful, reducing the courts to arenas of bribery and deceit. The critique is thus twofold, targeting both the societal structures and the individuals who have the capacity to alter these structures but choose complicity instead.

One profound dimension of Amos's economic critique is that it is deeply intertwined with the theological messages of the book. For Amos, economic injustice is not merely a social ill but a spiritual disgrace, obstructing the relationship between God and His people. This is evident in Amos 5:21-24, where God rejects the Israelites' religious ceremonies, stating: "Away with the noise of your songs! I will not listen to the music of your harps. But let justice roll on like a river, righteousness like a never-failing stream!" (NIV). Here, Amos equates true worship with acts of justice and righteousness, suggesting that genuine piety cannot coexist with economic exploitation and inequality. Neatly, this narrative redefines the spiritual landscape, emphasizing that divine acceptance is contingent upon the equitable treatment of all members of society.

Amos's critique raises essential questions about wealth and religious faithfulness, challenging any prosperity that is founded on inequality. It is a clear indictment of the dissonance between religious ritual and ethical practice. This transformative vision confronts believers with the enduring challenge to align spiritual devotion with socio-economic justice.

In conclusion, the economic inequality critique presented in the Book of Amos urges a fundamental re-evaluation of how wealth is perceived and utilized, urging both individual and collective responsibility. It stresses the biblical mandate for justice that transcends religious observance, advocating a socio-economic order reflective of God's justice. This potent message carries significant implications for contemporary discussions on economic disparity and serves as a timeless call for justice, ethical integrity, and compassion in societal governance.

Religious Hypocrisy and True Worship

The theme of religious hypocrisy and true worship is a pivotal aspect of the Book of Amos, reflecting the prophet's profound concern with the disparity between outward religious expressions and the internal moral and ethical responsibilities of the Israelites. Amos' ministry occurred during a time of apparent prosperity and stability in the northern kingdom of Israel, yet beneath the surface lay rampant injustices and moral decay. This setting provides a compelling backdrop against which Amos delivers divine indictments against the people's superficial religiosity and calls them to genuine worship and obedience.

Amos, a shepherd-turned-prophet, fiercely criticized the Israelites for maintaining external religious rituals while neglecting the ethical commandments that were integral to the covenant with Yahweh. This duality forms the crux of religious hypocrisy, wherein individuals engage in ceremonial practices devoid of sincere devotion or moral action. As Amos declares, "I hate, I despise your festivals, and I take no delight in your solemn assemblies" (Amos 5:21, NRSV).

Through such pointed declarations, Amos was condemning a religious culture that had become fixated on ritualistic observance rather than embodying the covenant's ethical mandates.

The central message of true worship emerges as Amos advocates for a form of worship that aligns with justice and righteousness. This is vividly captured in the oft-quoted verse, "But let justice roll down like waters, and righteousness like an ever-flowing stream" (Amos 5:24, NRSV). Here, Amos draws a stark contrast between hollow ritualism and the divine desire for justice and ethical living. The imagery of an ever-flowing stream conveys the notion of perpetual, active commitment to justice in society, as opposed to episodic religious ceremonies.

The critique of religious hypocrisy in Amos is deeply interwoven with social justice, extending the definition of true worship beyond personal piety to encompass fairness, equity, and compassion in societal structures. This intertwining of faith and ethics suggests that ritual acts, such as sacrifices and offerings, are rendered meaningless if detached from moral responsibility and commitment to rectify social wrongs. Amos's prophetic vision calls for a holistic practice of worship where ethical conduct is inextricable from spiritual devotion.

The historical context of the northern kingdom, with its social inequalities and economic exploitation, adds further depth to Amos's denunciation of religious hypocrisy. The affluent class's complicity in perpetuating oppression and injustice, all while engaging in religious observances, underscores a failure to grasp the covenant's comprehensive demands. In Amos's narrative, true worship cannot exist in isolation from societal transformation, reinforcing the integral relationship between divine commands and human action.

Furthermore, Amos highlights the dangers of complacency within religious practice. The prophet warns against a false sense of security derived from ritual observance, which lulls the populous into ignoring pressing social issues. This false piety is addressed in Amos 6:1, "Alas for those who are at ease in Zion," a rebuke of those who take refuge in empty ritual at the expense of authentic faith and justice. In doing so, Amos underscores the critical importance of self-examination and reform as components of sincere worship.

In conclusion, Amos's call to move beyond religious hypocrisy and embrace true worship resonates as a timeless message, confronting any community that falls prey to the allure of empty ritualism. The enduring legacy of Amos challenges believers to evaluate the authenticity of their worship by examining their commitment to justice, compassion, and ethical living. As such, the prophetic texts of Amos invite ongoing reflection and action, encouraging a form of worship that truly honors the divine through both reverence and righteousness.

The Book of Amos remains a compelling testimony to the belief that true worship transcends ritual, urging the faithful to seek a deeper, more substantive connection with the divine that is reflected in just and righteous societal conduct. Through such messages, Amos continues to inspire and provoke contemporary readers towards a faith that is both reflective and transformative.

The Hope and Promise of Restoration

In the tapestry of prophetic literature woven throughout the Hebrew Bible, the Book of Amos stands out for its unwavering focus on social justice and divine retribution. While much of the text fills readers with a sense of impending doom through prophetic oracles of judgment, it would be remiss to overlook the underlying thread of hope and promise of restoration that courses subtly yet powerfully through Amos's proclamations. This hope, though often overshadowed by the dominant themes of judgment and righteousness, reflects a profound theological principle: the relentless nature of divine mercy and the ultimate restoration that God promises to His people.

The latter portion of Amos introduces a transformative promise amid the foreboding admonitions. Amos 9:11-15 is particularly significant in this respect. It reads, "On that day

I will raise up the booth of David that is fallen and repair its breaches, and raise up its ruins, and rebuild it as in the days of old..." (ESV). The imagery of reconstruction and renewal offers a striking contrast to the preceding judgments, fostering hope for the future. Here, the "booth of David" symbolizes not just a physical restoration of Israel but a spiritual and communal renewal that aligns with God's eternal covenant.

This promise is discernible even through its metaphorical language—restoration isn't merely a return to the previous state but an elevation to what was intended in a divinely ordained reality. Interpretations, such as those offered by scholars like Shalom M. Paul in "Amos: A Commentary", emphasize that such restoration goes beyond political and territorial implications; it extends to a restorative act of divine grace that impacts every aspect of life, uniting divine justice with mercy (Paul, 1991).

While Amos meticulously critiques socioeconomic disparities and religious formalism earlier in the text, this vision of hope is comprehensive, covering both the individual and collective realms of existence. The restored kingdom represents not just the reestablishment of a political entity but the thriving of a just society in which righteousness and peace prevail—where the shortcomings highlighted in prior chapters are resolved through divine intervention as well as human repentance and transformation.

Furthermore, verse 9:13 evokes an idyllic reversal of fortunes for Israel: "The plowman shall overtake the reaper, and the treader of grapes him who sows the seed..." (ESV). This reversal signifies not only an economic abundance but also a divine blessing that transcends human capacity. It indicates a period when the natural order itself seems highly fruitful, reflecting a harmonious relationship between the people and their environment, emphasized in works such as James D. Nogalski's "The Book of the Twelve: Hosea–Jonah" (Nogalski, 2011).

In examining the profound implications of these promises, we note Amos's message that divine forgiveness is always accessible. Restoration in this sense carries a dual aspect: it is both a divine act and a human responsibility. Theologian Walter Brueggemann emphasizes in "Hopeful Imagination" that prophetic hope is "both a gift and a task" (Brueggemann, 1986). Thus, Amos's prophetic vision highlights not only divine action in history but also human participation through repentance and ethical reformation.

The promise of restoration in the Book of Amos is not an isolated eschatological event but deeply interwoven with the covenantal relationship between God and Israel. This dynamic relationship asserts that Israel's future is contingent upon its fidelity to the covenant, as seen in the rectification of societal and moral lapses critiqued earlier by Amos.

In conclusion, while the Book of Amos rigorously addresses issues of justice and consequences for moral failings, it is crucial to appreciate the profound hope embedded within its narrative structure. The vision of restoration exemplifies the breadth of God's redemptive plan, serving as both a conclusion to the current experiences of Israel and a prefiguration of Messianic expectations. By understanding this promise within the wider canonical context, one appreciates Amos not merely as a prophet of doom, but as a herald of renewal who frames divine judgment as a precursor to divine restoration.

Literary Structure and Style of Amos

Overview of the Book of Amos

The Book of Amos, an integral component of the Old Testament, stands as a profound testament to the religious and moral discourse of its era. Situated amongst the Minor Prophets, it constitutes a compelling collection of prophecies that were proclaimed against the backdrop of a tumultuous and morally complex period in Israel's history. Attributed to Amos, a shepherd from the region of Tekoa, this book is known for its vivid portrayal of social injustice, its fervent call for repentance, and its unwavering assertion of Yahweh's moral and ethical standards. This overview aims to provide a comprehensive understanding of the book's essence, scrutinizing its structure, main themes, and overarching messages.

The textual configuration of the Book of Amos is unique, reflecting a blend of literary styles that contribute to its compelling narrative. Scholars often categorize Amos into three primary structural units: the Oracles Against the Nations (Amos 1:1 – 2:16), the Words of Amos (Amos 3:1 – 6:14), and the Visions of Amos (Amos 7:1 – 9:15). Each of these sections encapsulates distinct facets of Amos's message, providing insights into the theological and social concerns of his prophetic ministry.

The Oracles Against the Nations establish the overarching theme of divine judgment. Amos begins by outlining Yahweh's condemnation of various nations surrounding Israel, including Damascus, Gaza, Tyre, Edom, Ammon, and Moab, for their transgressions against humanity (Amos 1:3-2:3). This section serves as both a precursor and a harsh reminder to Israel that divine justice is impartial, emphasizing the universality of God's moral expectations. The rhetorical structure employed here is noteworthy, utilizing a repetitive formula of indictment: "For three transgressions and for four, I will not revoke the punishment..." (*Amos 1:3, NRSV*), effectively building a crescendo towards an indictment of Israel and Judah themselves (Amos 2:4-16).

The Words of Amos further delineate Israel's failings, utilizing a series of oracles that reveal the nation's moral decay, characterized by greed, corruption, and religious hypocrisy. Central to this section is the motif of a divine lawsuit, where Yahweh, as the aggrieved party, lays bare the charges against Israel. Amos poignantly highlights their exploitation of the poor and neglect of justice, stating, "They sell the righteous for silver, and the needy for a pair of sandals" (*Amos 2:6, ESV*). This formulation deepens the theme of societal injustice, inviting the audience to reflect on the socioeconomic inequalities and the ethical obligations that have been neglected.

The section concludes with an urgent call for Israel to seek Yahweh, lest they encounter divine retribution (Amos 5:4-6). This plea underscores a central tenet of Amos's prophetic mission: repentance as imperative for survival and redemption. The literary form here is diverse, encompassing laments, visionary narratives, and direct exhortations.

The Visions of Amos encapsulate the eschatological elements of the prophet's message. This section presents Amos's vivid and unsettling visions – the locusts, the devouring fire, and the plumb line – each symbolizing an aspect of impending judgment. The narrative here shifts to an immediate, almost cinematic rendition of divine intervention, illustrating the ultimate consequences of iniquity if left unchecked (Amos 7:1-9:15). The resolution, however, pivots towards hope and restoration, culminating in a vision of a renewed and restored Israel under God's covenantal promises (Amos 9:11-15).

Overall, the Book of Amos offers a profound exploration of divine justice, emphasizing themes of accountability, restitution, and redemption. Its narrative, while grounded in historical context, evokes a timeless call for moral integrity, compassion, and social justice, rendering it an enduring testament to the ethical imperatives inherent in the prophetic tradition. This overview lays a foundation for deeper analyses to follow in this book, wherein each aspect of Amos is unraveled to shed light on its ongoing relevance and profound theological insights.

Historical Context and Authorship

The Book of Amos stands as a poignant testament within the corpus of biblical literature, intricately linked to its historical backdrop and the enigmatic figure of the prophet Amos himself. Understanding its historical context and authorship is key to unraveling the complexities and the powerful messages contained within this ancient text.

Amos, a shepherd-turned-prophet, flourished during a pivotal time in the history of ancient Israel. The eighth century BCE was marked by significant socio-economic changes and international tensions. It was a period when the Northern Kingdom, under the reigns of Jeroboam II (circa 793–753 BCE), experienced considerable prosperity and expansion. This era of affluence, however, was accompanied by stark social injustices, rampant corruption, and spiritual complacency among the people and their leaders. As noted by Cook (2008), "The time of Amos was one of Israel's greatest external successes but internal failures" (*Amos: Social Justice, p. 22*).

The historical setting provides crucial insights into the plight that Amos articulates with uncompromising vehemence. The socio-economic disparities were glaring, with wealth concentrated in the hands of an elite minority who thrived at the expense of the poor and marginalized. The legal and judicial systems, meant to uphold justice, were perverted and manipulated by those in power. Instead of acting as a society founded on divine precepts, Israel had deviated significantly from its covenantal obligations. This context is vital to appreciate the urgency and severity of Amos's prophetic messages.

Moreover, understanding the authorship of Amos enhances our comprehension of the text's literary style and theological nuances. The superscription in Amos 1:1 furnishes us with a brief yet invaluable insight, stating, "The words of Amos, who was among the shepherds of Tekoa..." This verse not only hints at his origin but also underscores his humble beginnings and outsider status. As Kim (2015) elucidates, "Amos emerges as a prophet with a distinct voice, grounded in rural authenticity, challenging the urban elite" (*Voices of the Prophets: Amos in Context, p. 34*).

Amos's origin in Tekoa, a village in Judah, positions him uniquely as a southerner called to prophesy against the Northern Kingdom of Israel. This cross-border mission is significant, suggesting that his prophecies transcend geographical and political boundaries, emphasizing a universal call to repentance and ethical conduct. It also raises intriguing questions about the reception of his message by an audience who may have viewed him as an outsider.

The extensive literary composition of the Book of Amos further reflects its multifaceted authorship. Scholars speculate that while Amos may have authored the core messages, subsequent redactions and expansions were likely carried out by disciples or later prophetic insertions. This claim is seen in the narrative continuity and stylistic elements that suggest multiple editorial hands. The text is punctuated with hymns and doxologies, lending a liturgical and reflective quality to the otherwise stark prophetic declarations.

In conclusion, the rich historical context and the conjectures surrounding authorship imbue the Book of Amos with profound depth and resonance. Amos's message, rooted in the socio-political realities of his time, challenges readers to reflect on themes of justice, divine judgment, and societal responsibilities. By examining these historical and authorial layers, we are better equipped to understand the enduring legacy of Amos's prophetic voice, which continues to speak powerfully to contemporary issues in our own time.

Language and Literary Devices

The Book of Amos, a cornerstone of the prophetic literature in the Hebrew Bible, stands out not only for its profound messages of social justice and divine judgment but also for its exceptional use of language and literary devices. This underappreciated aspect of Amos' writings reveals the depth and nuance through which the prophetic messages are conveyed. The intricate tapestry of language in Amos enables a profound and evocative communication of themes that resonate throughout the ages.

One of the most striking features of Amos' language is his adept use of **parallelism**, a key element in Hebrew poetry. Parallelism involves the juxtaposition of ideas or phrases that complement and enhance each other. For instance, Amos 5:24, "But let justice roll on like a river, righteousness like a never-failing stream," showcases synonymous parallelism, where the second line reinforces the idea presented in the first. This technique not only aids in the memorability of his words but also amplifies the emotional impact of the message (Alter, 1985).

Moreover, Amos employs **vivid imagery** to engage his audience's senses and intellect. His metaphors and similes are both relatable and vivid. Consider the imagery in Amos 4:1, where the prophet compares the indulgent women of Samaria to "cows of Bashan", creating a stark visual and moral critique. This use of pastoral imagery reflects both his background as a shepherd and the agrarian society of the time, grounding his prophetic vision in the everyday realities of his audience (Smith, 1998).

The **prophetic oracles** in Amos are frequently interwoven with **rhetorical questions**, serving to provoke thought and self-reflection among his listeners. In Amos 3:3-8, a series of rhetorical questions culminates in a powerful assertion of divine authority. This method not only engages the audience but also leads them to an inevitable logical conclusion that underscores the certainty and righteousness of God's judgment (Stuart, 1987).

Another significant device is the use of **irony**, which Amos expertly wields to highlight human folly and hypocrisy. In Amos 4:4-5, the prophet sarcastically invites the Israelites to continue their corrupted religious practices, knowing full well that their true purpose has been entirely subverted by self-serving agendas. This biting irony shames the audience, drawing attention to their moral and spiritual failings in a manner that straightforward rebuke might not achieve (Paul, 1991).

The deliberate use of **repetition** serves to emphasize critical themes, a technique evident in the lion's roar metaphor found in both Amos 1:2 and 3:8. The repeated imagery of a roaring lion – a representation of Yahweh's impending judgments – serves as a haunting reminder of the divine authority and power that underlie Amos' warnings. This not only reinforces the urgency of his message but also serves to engrain it deeply into the consciousness of his audience (Niehaus, 1992).

Furthermore, the **layered structure** of Amos's pronouncements, such as in the series of woes and laments (Amos 5:18-27), adds a dual dimension to his messages – at once both immediate and eschatological. The textual symmetry and pacing create a rhythm that captures the inevitability of judgment and the potential for repentance, offering both warning and hope (Mays, 1969).

The **economy of words** in the book is another notable element. Amos's concise language, often stripped to its bare essentials, packs a potent punch. This brevity ensures that his audience (both ancient and modern) remains focused on the core message without being distracted by superfluous details (Ward, 1963). Such precision in language enhances the timeless quality of his prophecies.

In conclusion, the Book of Amos, through its masterful language and literary devices, transcends mere historical narrative to impart timeless truths. The prophet's deft use of parallelism, imagery, rhetorical strategies, and structural inventions not only enriches the text but also amplifies the potency of its moral and theological implications. These literary elements work in concert to deliver a message that is as compelling today as it was in the 8th century BCE, urging audiences to introspection, repentance, and action. Such is the enduring power of Amos, a tribute to the literary richness and divine inspiration embedded within its text.

References:
Alter, R. (1985). *The Art of Biblical Poetry*. Harper & Row.
Smith, G. V. (1998). *Amos: A Commentary*. Westminster John Knox Press.

Stuart, D. (1987). *The New American Commentary: Hosea-Jonah*. Broadman & Holman Publishers.
Paul, S. M. (1991). *Amos: A Commentary on the Book of Amos*. Fortress Press.
Niehaus, J. J. (1992). *God at Sinai*. Zondervan.
Mays, J. L. (1969). *Amos: A Commentary*. Westminster John Knox Press.
Ward, J. M. (1963). *The Word Comes Alive: An Introduction to Old Testament Ethics*. Abingdon Press.

Structural Analysis of Amos

To truly appreciate the complexity and depth of the Book of Amos, it is essential to engage in a thorough structural analysis. Such an analysis reveals the intricate design embedded within the text, which augments both its message and its impact on the audience. The structural composition of Amos is not merely an aesthetic choice but serves a profound theological and rhetorical purpose.

The Book of Amos is fundamentally organized into three main sections: the oracles against the nations, the series of visions, and the words against Israel. Each section is meticulously constructed to fulfill its function within the overarching purpose of Amos' prophecy. Scholars such as Mays (1985) have long noted the deliberate composition within these divisions, seeing in them a framework that reflects Amos' prophetic agenda.

Amos 1:3–2:16 begins with a succession of oracles against neighboring nations, each introduced with the phrase "Thus says the Lord: for three transgressions... and for four..." (Amos 1:3, ESV). This formulaic repetition serves to build a cadence and expectation, drawing the audience in. As Carleton (1986) observes, the strategic escalation in these oracles draws attention inward, gradually focusing judgment upon Israel itself. This approach mirrors a classic rhetorical strategy wherein critique is extended to outsiders before tightening focus on the internal audience, maximizing the impact of the denunciation directed at Israel.

The section from Amos 3:1–6:14 comprises numerous judgment speeches against Israel. Within these chapters, the structure reveals a complex interplay of judgment, rationalization, and plea for repentance. Particularly noteworthy is the chiastic structure identified by scholars like Coote (1981), which sandwiches central themes of social justice and idolatry between introductory declarations of guilt and concluding visions of disaster. This mirroring technique underscores the cyclic nature of Israel's failures and the corresponding divine response.

Furthermore, the five visions in Amos 7:1–9:10 present a sophisticated ordering and thematic development. Beginning with the initial predictive vision and culminating in a vision of destruction, these visions not only serve a narrative progression but also emphasize Amos' prophetic authority. The rhetorical shift from dialogue between God and prophet (e.g., the vision of the locusts in Amos 7:1-3) to direct divine judgment (e.g., in Amos 9:1) accentuates the urgency and severity of the divine message.

Interwoven within these macro-structures are numerous micro-structures that demonstrate the remarkable skill of the author(s) of Amos. The use of parallelism, inclusio, and ring compositions is frequent, as noted in the works of Andersen (2001) and Wolff (1977). For example, consider the use of the repeated phrase in Amos 5:21-24: a juxtaposition of Israel's empty rituals against God's demand for justice and righteousness. This coupling of parallel imperatives creates a rhythmic force that drives home the prophet's core message.

The structural analysis of Amos also illuminates the book's unique literary style. For instance, the rhetorical questions scattered throughout (e.g., Amos 3:3-6) are not merely stylistic devices, but serve to engage the audience rhetorically, prompting introspection and moral reflection. Similarly, the employment of irony and paradox found in passages like Amos 4:4-5 challenges the audience's preconceptions and invites deeper engagement with the text's themes.

In conclusion, the structural examination of the Book of Amos reveals the text's intricate design and the deliberate craftsmanship with which its messages are delivered. Every component—from the order of prophecies and the arrangement of themes to the specific literary devices employed—

works collectively to deliver a potent theological message. Understanding this structure is vital for any serious study of Amos, offering insight into both its historical context and its lasting relevance.

Ultimately, the architectural depth of Amos fortifies its call to justice and righteousness, ensuring that its messages resonantly echo through time, challenging each new generation to reflect upon their own societal structures and moral standings.

Themes and Motifs in Amos

The Book of Amos is a rich tapestry of themes and motifs interwoven with the prophetic message delivered by Amos, a shepherd from Tekoa. This literary work, found among the Minor Prophets in the Hebrew Bible, is remarkable for its uncompromising stance on social justice, religious authenticity, and divine judgment. In examining its themes, we encounter a profound exploration of God's character, Israel's responsibilities, and the consequences of moral and spiritual complacency.

The overarching theme of justice is prevalent throughout Amos's prophecies. God's concern for justice is not merely judicial but deeply social, addressing the inequities and exploitation within society. Amos 5:24 is perhaps the most quoted verse illustrating this theme: "But let justice roll on like a river, righteousness like a never-failing stream" (NIV). This powerful imagery contrasts sharply with the superficial religious rituals of the Israelites, underscoring that true religious devotion must be accompanied by social justice.

Another significant motif is the theme of divine judgment. Amos does not shy away from pronouncing the imminent judgment on Israel and neighboring nations. The book opens with a series of oracles against the nations surrounding Israel, gradually intensifying to a direct rebuke of Israel itself. The rhetorical device of the "roaring lion" in Amos 1:2 serves as a metaphor for God's voice of impending doom: "The LORD roars from Zion and thunders from Jerusalem." This terrifying image sets the tone for the oracles, emphasizing the gravity of divine retribution in response to corruption and moral failings.

The theme of covenant faithfulness is interwoven with Amos's pronouncements of judgment. Unlike other nations, Israel is depicted as having a special covenant with Yahweh, which compounds their guilt because of their failure to live up to its stipulations. Amos 3:2 highlights this unique relationship: "You only have I chosen of all the families of the earth; therefore, I will punish you for all your sins." The covenant requires not just ritual observance but ethical living that reflects God's holiness and justice.

Religious hypocrisy is another motif addressed by Amos. The prophet sharply critiques the Israelites for their hollow religious ceremonies that were not accompanied by righteous living. In Amos 5:21-23, God expresses disdain for their festivals and assemblies, declaring, "Even though you bring me burnt offerings and grain offerings, I will not accept them." This divine rebuke underscores the dissonance between ritual acts and the lack of genuine ethical conduct, stressing the importance of sincerity and authenticity in worship.

Amos also presents a vision of hope and restoration amidst the backdrop of judgment. Although the book is primarily known for its stark warnings, it concludes with a promise of future restoration and blessing in Amos 9:11-15. These verses envision the restoration of the Davidic monarchy and the abundant prosperity of the land, offering a glimpse of redemption for a repentant people. It illustrates that God's ultimate intention is not destruction, but redemption and renewal.

The themes and motifs in Amos serve as a timeless reminder of the intricate balance between justice and mercy, judgment and hope. The book's rich prophetic language and powerful imagery challenge readers to reflect on their own societies and to consider the ways in which justice, faithfulness, and authentic worship may be pursued today. As such, Amos continues to resonate as a source of theological inquiry and moral reflection for contemporary readers, urging them to engage with the enduring call of God's righteousness and the pursuit of justice in a complex world.

In conclusion, the Book of Amos, through its diverse themes and motifs, communicates profound truths about divine justice, social ethics, and spiritual integrity. Its literary richness and prophetic depth invite continuous exploration and understanding, making it a pivotal text for both scholarly study and spiritual contemplation.

Prophetic Imagery and Symbolism

The exploration of prophetic imagery and symbolism within the Book of Amos unveils a tapestry of vivid illustrations, metaphors, and symbols, embodying the prophet's message with profound depth and conveyance. Amos, a shepherd and a dresser of sycamore trees, heralds a divine vision that transcends his origins, capturing both the imagination and the moral consciousness of his audience. To fully appreciate the intricate details of these symbolic elements, one must delve into the agricultural, societal, and spiritual milieu of ancient Israel.

One of the most prominent images in Amos is the depiction of Israel as a "ripe fruit," indicating impending judgment. In Amos 8:1-2, we encounter the phrase, "This is what the Lord God showed me: behold, a basket of summer fruit. And he said, 'Amos, what do you see?' And I said, 'A basket of summer fruit.' Then the Lord said to me, 'The end has come upon my people Israel; I will never again pass by them.'" The Hebrew word for "summer fruit" (*qayits*) phonetically resembles the word for "end" (*qets*), symbolically heralding the culmination of Israel's moral decay and the divine judgment that follows. This poignant use of imagery not only delivers a message of imminent doom but artistically bridges the auditory and visual spectrum of prophetic expression.

Another layer of symbolic imagery utilized by Amos is geological and geographical elements, such as earthquakes and the topographical features of Israel. In Amos 1:1, the text refers to an earthquake that serves as a temporal marker for his prophecies. This natural phenomenon represents upheaval, not just in the physical realm but also in the social and spiritual contexts of Israel. The imagery of a quaking earth underlines the instability and the seismic shifts required for societal repentance and renewal.

Furthermore, Amos employs imagery associated with divine retribution, notably through the motif of fire and destruction. The prophetic pronouncements in Amos frequently reference fire as a divine instrument of purification and judgment. For instance, in Amos 7:4, there is a vivid vision of the "Lord God calling for a judgment by fire, and it devoured the great deep and was eating up the land." The inferno symbolizes the consuming aspect of divine justice, reinforcing the seriousness of Israel's spiritual misdemeanors and the urgency of repentance.

Symbolism in Amos frequently extends beyond natural phenomena to include societal practices and religious observances, challenging their authenticity and integrity. Through rhetorical questions and metaphors, Amos critiques hollow worship and empty rituals, exposing their fraudulent nature. In Amos 5:21-24, God declares, "I hate, I despise your feasts, and I take no delight in your solemn assemblies... But let justice roll down like waters, and righteousness like an ever-flowing stream." Here, justice and righteousness are not just moral ideals but become powerful, flowing symbols of divine satisfaction and human obligation.

The potent imagery employed by Amos often conveys a call for social justice, resonating deeply with the overarching themes of economic disparity and moral corruption that pervade his prophecies. Amos's symbolism challenges both the layperson and the scholar to probe beyond surface interpretations and seek a deeper understanding of ethical responsibility as it pertains to divine mandates. This imagery serves as a prophetic lens, magnifying historical injustices and projecting them onto the canvas of timeless truths.

In summation, the prophetic imagery and symbolism within the Book of Amos paint a vivid portrait of divine communication, employing a rich palette of natural, social, and spiritual elements. Each image and symbol is meticulously crafted to engage the audience, provoking reflection, and compelling action. This profound use of imagery transforms Amos's message from mere historical account to a resonant call for righteousness, justice, and sincere devotion. Through

Amos's visionary narrative, believers and readers alike are invited to embark on a journey of introspection and transformation, a journey as vital today as it was in ancient Israel.

Rhetorical Strategies in Amos

The Book of Amos, traditionally classified among the Minor Prophets of the Hebrew Bible, stands out for its incisive and powerful rhetoric—a feature that has drawn considerable scholarly attention. In analyzing the rhetorical strategies used by the prophet Amos, it becomes clear that these strategies serve to sharpen his message, making it both compelling and memorable to his original audience and to readers across centuries.

At the core of Amos's rhetorical technique is the strategic use of repetition and parallelism. These tools are often employed to emphasize the unchanging nature of God's justice and the severity of Israel's transgressions. For instance, the rhythmical structure found in the opening chapters (Amos 1:3-2:16) utilizes repeated phrasing, "For three transgressions of [nation] and for four, I will not revoke the punishment," to methodically extend the ominous reach of divine judgment across various nations, ultimately centering on Israel. This literary device creates a crescendo of expectation, establishing a broader moral context before turning its critical focus on the audience itself—Israel.[1]

Amos also utilizes vivid imagery and metaphor to heighten the emotional impact of his messages. The book vividly portrays the disparity between the righteous and the unjust through agricultural and pastoral imagery, fitting for Amos's background as a shepherd and dresser of sycamore-fig trees. Notable passages such as Amos 4:1-3 depict the "cows of Bashan" as a metaphorical representation of the affluent and unjust women of Samaria who oppress the poor and crush the needy. Such imagery not only underscores the underlying moral critique but also serves to engage the audience's imaginations, ensuring the message is not easily dismissed.[2]

Another key rhetorical figure in the book is irony, which Amos employs to great effect. In Amos 5:21-24, the prophet skillfully exposes the futility of complacent worship devoid of justice and righteousness. He ironically presents God's rejection of Israel's sacrificial rituals in favor of moral and ethical living, culminating in the poignant call to "let justice roll down like waters, and righteousness like an ever-flowing stream." This dramatic juxtaposition between religious formalism and ethical substance is designed to provoke self-reflection and reconsideration among the listeners.[3]

Moreover, Amos frequently incorporates rhetorical questions and dialogical exchanges to engage his audience intellectually and morally. In Amos 3:3-8, a series of rhetorical questions leads to the logical climax: if God has spoken, the prophet must prophesy. This technique reinforces the necessity and inevitability of his mission, skillfully linking everyday observations with divine mandate. By engaging the audience in a logical sequence of thought, Amos effectively invites them to grapple with the implications of divine pronouncements being articulated.[4]

Additionally, Amos's use of pronouncement of coming disasters is structured to maintain a sense of urgency and immediacy. The oracles of judgment are terse and direct, often delivered with a sense of impending doom. This directness not only amplifies the severity of the message but also ensures clarity—unlike other prophetic works that may be more oblique, Amos leaves little room for ambiguity concerning the consequences of Israel's disobedience.[5]

A notable dimension of the rhetoric in Amos is the deployment of calls to listen, often marked by phrases such as "Hear this word..." (Amos 3:1; 4:1; 5:1). These injunctions serve a dual purpose: they demand the audience's attention while simultaneously reinforcing the authority of the prophet's message as divinely inspired. This commanding call to attention signals the significance of what follows, emphasizing the accountability of the audience to respond appropriately.[6]

In summary, the rhetorical strategies in the Book of Amos are varied and potent, encompassing repetition, metaphor, irony, rhetorical questioning, direct pronouncement, and deliberate calls to listen. Each serves to deepen the impact of Amos's prophecy, ensuring its durability as a source of theological and moral insight. Through these devices, Amos not only addressed his contemporaries with clarity and force but also crafted a message that continues to resonate powerfully with audiences today, making it a timeless call to justice and righteousness.

[1] Mays, J. L. (1969). Amos: A Commentary. Philadelphia: Westminster John Knox Press.

[2] Paul, S. M. (1991). Amos: A Commentary on the Book of Amos. Minneapolis: Fortress Press.

[3] Andersen, F. I., & Freedman, D. N. (1989). Amos: A New Translation with Introduction and Commentary. New York: Yale University Press.

[4] Wolff, H. W. (1977). Joel and Amos: A Commentary on the Books of the Prophets Joel and Amos. Philadelphia: Fortress Press.

[5] Hayes, J. H. (1988). Amos the Eighth-Century Prophet: His Times and His Preaching. Nashville: Abingdon Press.

[6] Jeremias, J. (1998). The Book of Amos in Its Social and Cultural Contexts. Sheffield: Sheffield Academic Press.

The Role of Oracles and Visions

The Book of Amos, a cornerstone of prophetic literature in the Hebrew Bible, provides rich insight into the divine messages conveyed through the prophet Amos. Central to understanding the complexity and depth of this book is the role of oracles and visions, which form a significant portion of Amos's communication. These elements not only underscore the divine source of the prophet's messages but also engage the audience in a narrative that is both vivid and profound.

Oracles, in the prophetic tradition, serve as the authoritative statements of divine will. In the Book of Amos, they are presented in a manner that reflects both condemnation and hope, echoing the broader thematic structure of judgment and eventual restoration found throughout prophetic literature. The oracles of Amos often begin with the formulaic "Thus says the Lord," a typical introductory phrase that authenticates the message as divine in origin. These declarations cover a range of topics, predominantly focusing on injustices pertaining to social and religious transgressions. Amos 1:3, for example, opens with such an oracle, "Thus says the Lord: For three transgressions of Damascus, and for four, I will not revoke the punishment…" (ESV), indicating a common pattern that amplifies the gravity of the offences.

While the oracles often carry a tone of impending judgment, they also reveal a crucial aspect of prophetic literature: the capacity for repentance and change. The conditional nature of the prophetic pronouncements hints at divine mercy—a theme subtly woven throughout Amos's messages. Scholarship frequently highlights Amos 5:14-15, which calls for seeking good and not evil, promising life as a reward for such actions. The duality of judgment and mercy invites readers to contemplate the moral responsibilities inherent in the prophetic call.

Visions, another significant component of Amos's literary style, enrich the narrative by offering symbolic imagery that complements the oracles. The visions in Amos, notably chapters 7 through 9, depict vivid scenarios that communicate God's intentions and the potential consequences for Israel. For instance, the vision of the plumb line (Amos 7:7-8) serves as a metaphor for divine judgment, illustrating Israel's moral imbalance. This vision succinctly encapsulates the principle of divine assessment, urging the nation to realign with God's standards.

Each vision in Amos serves a distinct function, yet collectively they reinforce the central messages of accountability and divine sovereignty. The imagery associated with these visions is not merely artistic but deeply theological. As noted by scholars such as James L. Mays, these visions invite the audience to engage in introspection, "challenging them to discern their own alignment with divine will," thereby making these passages timeless in their relevance (Mays, J. L. "Amos: A Commentary," pp. 126-131).

Moreover, the interplay of oracles and visions in Amos is emblematic of the broader prophetic narrative—a balance of divine justice and mercy conveyed through both declarative and visual means. This dual approach not only strengthens the rhetorical impact but also enriches the theological discourse of the book. As a result, the text of Amos becomes a powerful medium through which the dynamics of divine-human interaction are articulated, offering multifaceted insight into the prophetic tradition.

Further examination of these elements underscores the importance of contextual and literary analysis in fully appreciating the Book of Amos. Through the intricate dance of oracles and visions, Amos not only delivers a powerful critique of contemporary injustices but also, as echoed by Marvin A. Sweeney in his studies, "provides enduring lessons on moral and ethical imperatives that transcend time" (Sweeney, M. A. "The Twelve Prophets," Vol. 1, p. 154).

In conclusion, the oracles and visions within the Book of Amos serve as pivotal mechanisms through which the prophet illuminates the heart of divine concerns, challenges complacency, and calls for transformation. Their study offers profound insights into the prophetic mission, inviting ongoing reflection on the timeless themes of justice, mercy, and righteousness.

Poetic Forms in Amos

In the examination of the Book of Amos, a profound understanding of the poetic forms used within the text reveals the intricacy and depth of this prophetic work. Amos, a minor prophet, utilizes various poetic forms to convey his messages of divine judgment, social justice, and moral imperatives. This undercurrent of poetic eloquence not only aids in engaging the audience but also underscores the gravity of the prophecies delivered. The exploration of these poetic forms is crucial to appreciate the literary artistry and the rhetorical power endemic to Amos's delivery.

One of the most prominent poetic structures in Amos is parallelism, a fundamental characteristic of Hebrew poetry. Parallelism in Amos frequently takes the form of synonymous, antithetic, and synthetic parallelism, each serving a distinct purpose in conveying the prophet's message. Synonymous parallelism subtly reinforces Amos's points by repeating similar ideas in successive lines. For instance, in Amos 5:24— "But let justice roll down like waters, and righteousness like an ever-flowing stream"—the synonymous nature of justice and righteousness, as well as waters and a stream, emphasizes the need for unwavering divine principles in human conduct.

Similarly, antithetic parallelism highlights stark contrasts, a technique often employed by Amos to reflect moral binaries. An example can be found in Amos 5:14-15, where the juxtaposition of good and evil serves as a moral compass for the people: "Seek good, and not evil, that ye may live." This serves as a reminder of the conditional nature of divine favor, predicated upon adherence to moral righteousness.

Furthermore, Amos incorporates chiasmus, an inverted parallelism that mirrors ideas to emphasize certain truths within the layered structure of a passage. This structure creates a reflective space for contemplation and emphasizes the covenantal relationship between Yahweh and His people. A chiastic structure is discernible in Amos 3:3-8, underscoring the irrevocability of the Lord's decrees: the structure climaxes with the prophetic assertion in verse 8, "The lion hath roared, who will not fear? The Lord GOD hath spoken, who can but prophesy?" Here, the imagery of the lion roaring encapsulates the inevitability and the divine authority of the prophetic word.

In addition, Amos demonstrates sophisticated usage of imagery and metaphor, elevating the poetic dimension of the text. One of the most vivid imagistic techniques is the "basket of summer fruit" in Amos 8:1-2, symbolizing the transitory prosperity of Israel that is ripe for divine judgment. This metaphor is expanded upon with the Lord's pronouncement: "The end is come upon my people Israel." The visual metaphor effectively bridges the tangible with the eschatological, urging immediate introspection and reform.

The employment of rhetorical questions further reflects Amos's poetic dexterity, as they serve to provoke contemplation and self-reflection among his listeners. These questions punctuate the discourse and force the audience to internalize the implications of their societal transgressions. For example, Amos 3:3-6 contains a series of rhetorical questions that build upon each other to lead into a final divine explanation, reinforcing the prophet's role and the nature of the divine message imparted: "Can two walk together, except they be agreed?"

Amos's poetic expression is enriched by the presence of lamentations and hymnic passages, where a shift in tone from immediacy to reflective mourning can be found. These lamentations, such as those in Amos 5:1-2, "Hear ye this word which I take up against you, even a lamentation, O house of Israel," create a deliberate pause within the text, allowing the audience to reflect on the ruin and restoration dichotomy. This appeal to emotion ensures that the call for repentance is not only understood cognitively but felt intimately.

The poetics of Amos do not merely embellish the message but are integral to the communication of the prophet's divine mission. These literary forms, when dissected, illuminate the complexities and intensities of Amos's prophetic declaration, anchoring his message firmly within the traditions of Hebrew poetic expression. Understanding these forms allows a deeper appreciation of the rhetorical force and enduring relevance of the Book of Amos, cementing its place as a cornerstone of prophetic literature.

As we delve into the poetic mastery of Amos, it becomes clear that this prophetic book is much more than a collection of oracles and visions. It is a carefully structured, artistically driven dialogue with the divine, inviting successive generations to reflect on the timeless call for justice and righteousness.

Comparative Analysis with Other Prophetic Books

The prophetic book of Amos stands as a remarkable testament of the ancient wisdom woven throughout the Hebrew Bible. To fully appreciate the literary structure and style of Amos, a comparative analysis with other prophetic books becomes essential. By examining key texts such as Isaiah, Jeremiah, Ezekiel, and Hosea, we can elucidate the unique features and common motifs that make Amos stand out as a distinct voice in the biblical prophetic tradition.

Amos uses a distinct literary style that incorporates vivid imagery, rhetorical questions, and potent use of irony. The comparative analysis situates these elements within a broader prophetic context. For instance, Isaiah's eloquent poetry and grand visions contrast with the often blunt and straightforward messages found in Amos. While Isaiah presents a divine vision with sophisticated linguistic beauty,

Amos conveys God's displeasure with terse and powerful declarations.

Jeremiah, often termed as the 'weeping prophet,' similarly shares the theme of pronounced judgments but utilizes a heartfelt and emotional tone. His lamentations over Israel's fate and his personal struggles permeate the narrative structure of his book. Amos, contrastingly, is hardly found wrestling with personal anguish; instead, he presents divine judgment with a certain resoluteness that lacks personal agony on display in Jeremiah.

Ezekiel's book, filled with bizarre and symbolic visions, makes for an intriguing case study next to Amos. While both convey God's messages with the assurance of impending doom, Ezekiel relies heavily on allegory and intricate symbols, such as the dry bones and the idolatrous temple. Amos, pragmatic in approach, roots his prophetic voice in real-world imagery — lion's roars and summer fruit — to underscore the immediacy and reality of God's judgment.

Hosea offers another foil for Amos's style. Known for his heartbreaking metaphor of unfaithfulness to characterize Israel's relationship with God, Hosea's marriage narrative provides a deep, almost tender look at divine compassion despite human infidelity. This narrative device is absent in Amos, where the emphasis is more consistently on ethical breaches and societal injustices. Amos's stark warnings and calls for justice often appear devoid of the relational dynamics so prominent in Hosea.

A recurring motif observable within these prophetic books is the confrontation of social inequities and spiritual infidelity, yet each book approaches these motifs in a unique manner. Amos's insistence on social justice — "But let justice roll down as waters, and righteousness as a mighty stream" (Amos 5:24) — finds echoes in Isaiah's and Micah's similar calls for societal reform. However, Amos's denunciations come with unrelenting intensity, framing ethical norms as inseparable from divine commandments.

Additionally, the employment of oracles serves as a thematic bridge across these prophetic texts. The "oracles against the nations" in Amos (Amos 1-2) share structural elements with corresponding sections in Isaiah and Jeremiah. These oracles lay bare the national and international scope of God's judgment, presenting a universal moral order that reinforces the covenantal theology inherent in Israel's understanding of God.

The frequent usage of rhetorical strategies such as repetition and parallelism aligns Amos with classical Hebrew poetic techniques, yet the terse, indictive approach is distinctively his own. Through comparison, we observe Amos's economical use of language as strikingly effective in its communicative immediacy, particularly when juxtaposed with the often elaborate and extended oracles of his prophetic peers.

Theological implications drawn from such comparative analyses underscore the multifaceted dimensions of prophetic ministry, where each prophet's message is shaped by context, audience, and divine inspiration. Amos's contribution lies significantly in his resolute call for justice and unwavering articulation of divine ethical standards, presenting a God who demands moral integrity above ritual performance.

Thus, while Amos shares common threads with other prophets, his distinctive voice is amplified through comparative literary analysis. The starkness of his proclamations, the practical immediacy of his imagery, and his unwavering focus on justice offer a vibrant, unembellished, and compelling addition to the corpus of biblical prophecy. Amos challenges readers across the ages, calling them to action with words that resonate with vitality and urgency. This, indeed, is the enduring contribution of Amos to the prophetic literature of the Bible.

Theological Implications and Interpretations

The Book of Amos, nestled among the prophetic texts of the Old Testament, stands as a potent testament to the theological underpinnings that characterize the Hebrew tradition. The work is not just a collection of stern reprimands or a blistering critique of societal injustices; rather, it is a rich tapestry of theological nuances that offer profound insights into the nature of God, the function of prophecy, and the responsibilities of humanity.

At the heart of Amos is a vivid portrayal of God as a deity who is both just and righteous. These attributes form the cornerstone of Amos's theology, where divine justice is not abstract but intimately tied to social behavior and ethical conduct. Amos articulates a vision of God who is deeply invested in the moral order of society. The prophet's insistent call for justice and righteousness reflects a theological conviction that God demands these virtues from His people. As Richard S. Cripps writes, "The moral order is not merely a social construct, but a divine imperative" (Cripps, _Amos and the Popular Prophets_, p. 87).

Amos introduces an understanding of God that transcends national boundaries and ethnic considerations. This universalistic aspect is encapsulated in the opening of the book, where judgment is pronounced not only on Israel but on the surrounding nations as well (Amos 1:3–2:16). The book argues that divine accountability is expected of all nations, underscoring a theological perspective that God's sovereignty and expectations extend beyond Israel alone. This is particularly significant because it challenges the contemporary understanding of a nationalistic deity confined to a single people, expanding instead toward a more globally inclusive interpretation of God's intervention in human affairs.

Equally compelling in Amos is the tension between divine judgment and divine mercy. Scholars have long debated the book's apparent emphasis on punishment over forgiveness. However, the ultimate aim of divine judgment in Amos is remedial rather than punitive. Even amidst vivid oracles of impending doom, there are glimpses of hope and restoration, notably in the concluding verses of the book (Amos 9:11-15). Here, the theological implication is that judgment serves as a redemptive tool to bring about repentance and renewal. As John Barton observes, "The very expression of wrath is a facet of God's enduring love—a strange, albeit integral, part of His covenantal fidelity" (Barton, _The Theology of Amos_, p. 132).

The prophetic function in Amos can be understood as an extension of God's immanence. Amos acts as a conduit for divine communication, embodying the belief that God is actively engaged in the world through His chosen messengers. The authority of the prophetic voice is derived directly from this divine commission, which positions the prophet as an intermediary who brings the divine will to bear upon the temporal world. This is succinctly captured in Amos's own rebuttal to Amaziah, the priest of Bethel, affirming his divine calling: "I was no prophet, nor a prophet's son, but I was a herdsman... and the LORD took me from following the flock, and the LORD said to me, 'Go, prophesy to my people Israel'" (Amos 7:14-15).

A further theological impulse in the book is the concept of the 'Day of the Lord', a recurring theme in the prophetic literature, which Amos reinterprets as a day of gloom for Israel rather than triumph (Amos 5:18-20). This reinterpretation serves as a stark warning against complacency and underscores the serious nature of divine involvement where assumed privilege does not equate to guaranteed favor. Theologically, this challenges prevailing eschatological assumptions and invites a re-evaluation of what constitutes divine favor.

Moreover, Amos speaks to the relational dynamics between God and His people, encapsulating the covenantal framework that demands both accountability and reciprocal responsibility. The frequent use of covenantal language throughout the text underscores the theological premise that Israel's chosen status is not a shield against divine scrutiny but rather a heightened expression of divine expectations. As Walther Eichrodt articulates, "The covenant is not merely a historical relic, but a living reality that demands ethical and spiritual fidelity" (Eichrodt, _Theology of the Old Testament_, Vol.1, p. 273).

In conclusion, the Book of Amos offers a profound theological narrative that presents God as a just, universal, and relational deity. These theological themes are intricately woven into the fabric of Amos, providing insights that extend beyond historical or literary analysis, inviting readers to reflect on the enduring nature of divine justice and mercy. Ultimately, Amos challenges its audience to engage with a God who is actively involved in the moral compass of the world, urging a response that aligns with divine righteousness and compassionate justice.

Modern Literary Criticism Perspectives

Modern literary criticism provides a tapestry of perspectives through which the intricacies of biblical texts like the Book of Amos can be unraveled and appreciated with renewed depth. Scholars have employed various critical methodologies to explore the literary and rhetorical craftsmanship present in Amos, revealing a multiplicity of interpretative angles that both challenge and enrich traditional readings.

One prominent modern critical approach is the **narrative criticism** that focuses on analyzing the story and its components in the text of Amos. Though not a narrative in the traditional sense, Amos consists of a series of speeches and visions that together form a coherent prophetic discourse. Narrative criticism often highlights the progression and relationship between these speeches, enabling a clearer understanding of Amos's message and the intended impact on his audience.

Another significant angle is the application of **literary structuralism**. This lens examines the structural underpinnings of Amos, exploring how its internal architecture influences meaning. Structuralists might dissect the parallelism, chiasmus, and other literary structures to elucidate how these tools contribute to thematic development or underline key messages of social justice and divine judgment that Amos is renowned for. For instance, the symmetrical patterns in Amos's composition highlight the dual themes of destruction and hope, offering a balance that is essential for a comprehensive hermeneutic approach.

Additionally, **reader-response criticism** grants attention to the active role of the reader in interpreting the text. In the context of Amos, this involves understanding how contemporary and historical audiences receive and emotionally engage with the vivid imagery and symbolism. Reader-response critics argue that the meaning of Amos emerges dynamically, created by the interaction between text and reader, an idea supported by Fish (1980), who asserts that "the reader's role is essential in actualizing a text's potential meaning". This perspective encourages modern readers to bring their personal experiences into dialogue with the text, thereby generating diverse interpretations that may align with or expand established theological understandings.

The disciplined field of **socio-rhetorical criticism** pays particular attention to the social, cultural, and rhetorical dimensions that inform the prophetic proclamations in Amos. This approach analyzes how the social realities of 8th century BCE Israel are mirrored in Amos's rhetoric, connecting the prophet's calls for justice with the broader societal structures of his time. Robbins (1996) emphasizes that rhetoric in biblical texts like Amos is designed not just to inform, but to transform the audience, a goal made manifest through Amos's compelling cries for repentance and change.

Moreover, the rising interest in **feminist criticism** offers a distinctive take on Amos by questioning the representation of gender and power dynamics within the text. Feminist scholars might investigate the patriarchal context of Amos's prophecies and examine how the text represents gendered identities and roles. By exploring these nuances, this criticism opens up dialogues about justice and equality, resonating with the overarching social justice themes found within Amos.

Finally, **postcolonial criticism** offers insights into the power dynamics and imperial influences that Amos addresses. Postcolonial critics seek to deconstruct how empire, dominance, and subjugation are highlighted within the narrative and language of Amos. This critical approach is essential in recognizing how prophetic denunciations serve not only as theological pronouncements but also as subversive critiques against prevailing hegemonies, thus providing a voice to the oppressed.

In embracing these modern critical perspectives, readers of Amos are afforded a richer understanding that not only acknowledges but also celebrates the complexity and multifaceted nature of this prophetic book. Each perspective furnishes distinctive lenses that, when woven together, form an expansive interpretative fabric that enhances both academic and devotional engagements with the text.

Citations:
Fish, S. (1980). Is There a Text in This Class?: The Authority of Interpretive Communities. Harvard University Press.
Robbins, V. K. (1996). Exploring the Texture of Texts: A Guide to Socio-Rhetorical Interpretations. Trinity Press International.

Prophecies of Judgment and Warnings

Historical Context and Background of Amos's Prophecies

The Book of Amos stands as a pivotal text within the tapestry of the Hebrew Bible, offering both a profound prophetic vision and a scathing critique of social injustices. Before delving into the intricate messages of Amos, it is imperative to first comprehend the historical context in which these prophecies were proclaimed. The historical backdrop of Amos's prophecies is not merely a passive setting but a vibrant canvas against which the divine truths unfold. Understanding the socioeconomic, religious, and political milieu of 8th century BCE Northern Israel is crucial for appreciating the potency and urgency of Amos's message.

Historically, Amos's prophecies were set during the reign of King Jeroboam II of Israel, who reigned from approximately 786 to 746 BCE. This era was marked by a period of unparalleled prosperity and stability for the Northern Kingdom. The Assyrian Empire, which had posed a significant threat in preceding decades, was temporarily weakened, allowing Israel to flourish economically and expand its territorial boundaries (Coogan, 2009). Under Jeroboam II's rule, Israel achieved a semblance of a golden age, reminiscent of the time of King Solomon.

However, beneath this veneer of prosperity and peace lay a society steeped in moral decay and social inequality. Wealth was increasingly concentrated in the hands of the elite, while the poor and marginalized were subjected to systemic oppression and exploitation. The affluent enjoyed lavish lifestyles, as evidenced by archaeological findings of opulent homes, while the downtrodden suffered injustices such as debt slavery and land dispossession (Smith, 1989). The religious life of Israel, too, was compromised, characterized by a syncretistic worship that blended elements of Yahwism with Canaanite religious practices, thereby violating the covenantal relationship with Yahweh.

Amos himself hailed from the southern kingdom of Judah, specifically from the small village of Tekoa. His background as a shepherd and a dresser of sycamore-fig trees is significant; it lent him a vantage point distinct from that of the religious and political elites in Israel. Unlike professional prophets associated with official temples, Amos was an outsider, unencumbered by institutional allegiances, which allowed him to speak boldly and authentically (Andersen & Freedman, 1989).

The socioeconomic disparities and religious corruption of the time provided the predicament that Amos fiercely condemned. His prophecies targeted not only the elites who perpetrated injustices but also the broader social structures that enabled such inequities to perpetuate. The central tenets of Amos's message resonate around themes of justice and righteousness, central to which is the idea that true worship of God is inseparable from the ethical treatment of fellow humans (Amos 5:24).

The prophetic utterances of Amos gained urgency in the light of the geopolitical threats looming on the horizon. The revitalized Assyrian Empire, under rulers like Tiglath-Pileser III, posed an existential threat to Israel. Amos foresaw the impending doom that would befall Israel due to its moral failings and failure to heed his divine warnings. His prophecies were not merely predictions of disaster but served as calls for repentance and social reform, albeit ones that went unheeded by the majority of his contemporaries.

In conclusion, the historical context and background of Amos's prophecies are not mere footnotes to his message but rather its essential substratum. By understanding the economic prosperity juxtaposed with social injustices, the religious syncretism, and the external threats of Amos's era, modern readers can better appreciate both the historical significance and the enduring relevance of the prophet's message. The Book of Amos, therefore, serves as both a mirror reflecting the societal issues of its time and a timeless beacon guiding current and future generations towards justice and righteousness.

References:

Coogan, M. D. (2009). *A Brief Introduction to the Old Testament: The Hebrew Bible in Its Context*. Oxford University Press.

Smith, M. S. (1989). *The Early History of God: Yahweh and Other Deities in Ancient Israel*. Harper & Row.

Andersen, F. I., & Freedman, D. N. (1989). *Amos: A New Translation with Introduction and Commentary*. Yale University Press.

The Role of the Prophet: Amos's Call and Mission

The book of Amos, nested within the collection known as the Minor Prophets, presents a profound narrative of prophetic vocation and societal admonition. Central to this narrative is the role of Amos himself, who steps into the pages of Scripture not as a seasoned prophet but as a shepherd and dresser of sycamore trees from Tekoa, a small town in Judah. His call to prophecy is marked by a profound simplicity and authenticity that underscores the divine sovereignty and purposeful disruption inherent in the prophetic mission.

Amos's commissioning stands in stark contrast to the more elaborate call narratives of prophets like Isaiah and Jeremiah. Whereas these prophets recount grandiose visions and divine touch, Amos presents his story with a disarming humility. In Amos 7:14-15, he declares, "I was neither a prophet nor a prophet's son, but I was a shepherd, and I also took care of sycamore-fig trees. But the Lord took me from tending the flock and said to me, 'Go, prophesy to my people Israel.'" This account emphasizes the abrupt divine initiative that disrupts Amos's simple pastoral life, a theme that underscores the divine election and empowerment over human qualification.

The mission to which Amos is called is one laden with divine instruction and solemn responsibility. His task is not the result of inherited tradition or professional lineage, but a direct mandate from God. This underscores a fundamental tenet in prophetic literature: the centrality of the divine word as the source of authority and mission. Amos, obedient to this call, ventures from the southern kingdom of Judah to the northern kingdom of Israel during the reign of Jeroboam II, a period marked by political stability and economic prosperity, yet rife with moral and religious decay.

The book of Amos reflects a complex interplay between Amos's divinely appointed mission and the socio-religious environment of Israel. Israel's socio-economic prosperity conceals a deep-seated corruption, inequality, and neglect of covenantal responsibilities. Against this backdrop, Amos emerges as a divine emissary, tasked with confronting the complacency of the nation's affluent class, denouncing their injustices, and calling them back to covenant fidelity.

The primary vocation of a prophet, as illustrated by Amos, involves two overarching duties: to convey divine judgment and to call for repentance. Amos's oracles resonate with an urgency and clarity meant to pierce the hardened hearts of their recipients. His message is one of impending judgment—a theme persistently echoed through metaphors and symbolic actions such as the plumb line and baskets of ripe fruit. These symbols articulate the themes of falling short of divine expectation and imminent destruction (Amos 7:7-8; 8:2).

What is particularly unique to Amos is his integration of ethical monotheism with economic and social justice. This is evident as he ceaselessly condemns the luxury and exploitation by the elites within Israelite society: "They trample on the heads of the poor as on the dust of the ground and deny justice to the oppressed" (Amos 2:7). Such statements reflect the heart of Amos's mission: to reveal how spiritual apostasy is intrinsically connected to societal injustice and to urge a return to justice and righteousness—foundational principles of the Mosaic covenant.

Moreover, Amos's role transcends mere denunciation to serve as a prophetic intermediary of hope conditional upon repentance. Despite the foreboding tone of judgment, Amos's mission holds a redemptive potential propelled by an underlying call to communal and individual transformation. In this respect, Amos's proclamations echo the broader theological narrative of conditionality seen throughout the Hebrew Bible: that divine judgment can be averted and hope can actually blossom if genuine repentance and reform occur.

The legacy of Amos's mission has profound implications for understanding the nature of prophetic ministry. Amos exemplifies that the prophetic office is one that demands courage in the face of opposition, faithfulness to an uncompromising divine commission, and a relentless pursuit of justice. His story serves as a witness to the transformative power of the prophetic word and its relevance across the ages, challenging communities to align with the divine vision of justice and compassion.

Amos's mission challenges contemporary interpreters to consider the roles of divine agency and human responsibility in the unfolding saga of justice and righteousness. Thus, Amos not only stands as a historical figure within the prophetic tradition but also as an enduring voice calling out for integrity and reform in every age. It is through Amos's example that we are invited to reflect on the timeless question: how does one live justly in an unjust world under the sovereign call of the divine?

The Nations Under Judgment: Surrounding Countries

The Book of Amos provides a poignant and unflinching narrative addressing the nations surrounding Israel, which sets the stage for Amos's broader messages of societal and divine justice. Situated during the reigns of Uzziah in Judah and Jeroboam II in Israel, this 8th-century BCE prophet delivers pronouncements not only to Israel but to its neighbors—Damascus, Gaza, Tyre, Edom, Ammon, and Moab—foreshadowing the judgment that awaits them. These countries, geographically close and culturally intertwined with Israel, were judged for their transgressions, serving as a prelude to the prophet's ultimate message directed towards Israel.

The initial chapters of Amos (Amos 1:3-2:3) meticulously enumerate the failings of these nations. As this segment underlines, the oracles against the nations underscore the widespread nature of moral decay and hold each accountable for their distinct iniquities. Biblical scholars highlight that Amos employs a specific rhetorical formula: "For three transgressions...and for four, I will not revoke the punishment", indicating a cumulative sin that has reached the point of divine intervention (Amos 1:3 ESV).

Damascus is the first nation to face Amos's rebuke. Known for its violence against Gilead, the capital of Aram (modern-day Syria) receives divine condemnation for thrashing Gilead with implements of iron. Historical evidence, supported by the archaeological findings, suggests the fervency and brutality in these campaigns that likely caused significant human and resource devastation. The prophecy foretells the destruction of Damascus's palaces and the captivity of its people, concluding with the breaking of the gate bar of Damascus, highlighting its eventual defeat and subjugation (Amos 1:3-5).

Following Damascus, Gaza, representing the Philistine pentapolis, is chided primarily for its slave trading—delivering vast groups of captives to Edom. This act is depicted as a breach of human compassion and ethical standards. By targeting coastal trading hubs like Gaza, Amos castigates their role in a commerce that enabled human suffering, thus predicting cities turning into ruins and their ruling dynasties falling (Amos 1:6-8).

Continuing his oratorial charge, Amos's prophetic vision turns to Tyre. As a pivotal maritime trader and ally of Israel through the reigns of David and Solomon (1 Kings 5), Tyre's betrayal through slave trade towards Edom is chastised, breaching ancient covenants of brotherhood and alliance (Amos 1:9-10). This infraction underlines the theme of broken alliances and mutual betrayal.

Edom stands condemned for its relentless domestic violence, characterized by an "unceasing anger", symbolizing hatred and vengeance against brother nations, notably Israel (Amos 1:11-12). Archeological insights on Edomite settlements and incantations in trans-Jordan regions explore the age-old animosities rooted in Esau's legacy borne out within the tribal memories of Edom and Israel.

The following oracle targets Ammon for their "ripping open the pregnant women of Gilead," reflecting extreme acts of cruelty for territorial expansion (Amos 1:13-15). The devastation and displacement strategies are mirrored through archaeological digs revealing evidences of raids across ammonite domains, signifying tangible manifestations of Amos's messages.

Finally, Moab's judgment rests upon desecration and relentless retribution (Amos 2:1-3). The act of burning the king of Edom's bones into lime points towards intense inter-tribal hostilities and sacrilegious acts, showcasing profound disregard for human dignity and divine laws. The resultant prophecy envisions Moab consumed within the flames of its own making.

Through the oracles against the nations, Amos transcends the immediate cultural context, critiquing not merely the historical foes of Israel but illustrating a universal standard of justice. This aspect of Amos's message often resonates within modern discourses on ethics and international justice, particularly with regards to human rights violations and systemic injustices.

Most notably, these prophecies delineate Amos as a harbinger of divine justice that pivots upon the actions and ethics across nations, reflecting a biblical paradigm wherein human relations, rooted in moral and spiritual realms, are determinant of divine favor or wrath. As modern readers delve into these texts, they find the enduring relevance of ethical accountability, collective responsibility, and the perennial call for justice that transcends time, echoing within the contemporary fabric of global societies.

Israel's Transgressions: Social Injustice and Idolatry

The prophet Amos, a shepherd and sycamore fig farmer, became a pivotal voice in the 8th century BCE, delivering compelling admonitions to the Northern Kingdom of Israel. His central message focused on judgment and the urgent need for repentance, primarily due to Israel's rampant social injustices and idolatry. In this context, Amos's prophecies starkly highlighted two main transgressions: the exploitation of the poor and marginalized, and the deviation from monotheistic worship.

Amos's contemporaneous Israel was characterized by economic prosperity, which, paradoxically, intensified social disparity and moral corruption. Through Amos, God condemned the Israelites' refusal to uphold the ethical demands of their covenant with Yahweh, notably derailing into moral decay as articulated in Amos 2:6-7: "They sell the righteous for silver, and the needy for a pair of sandals. They trample on the heads of the poor as upon the dust of the ground and deny justice to the oppressed." (NIV) This indictment accentuates the commodification of justice, where wealth prioritized over human dignity, signaling profound systemic exploitation.

The book of Amos serves as a resounding critique against societal complacency in the face of such injustices. The opulence of the ruling class, as criticized in Amos 3:15, "I will tear down the winter house along with the summer house; the houses adorned with ivory will be destroyed and the mansions will be demolished," (NIV) represents the hollow, superficial security that prosperity brought—a prosperity built on the backs of the impoverished. This period witnessed the fortification of socioeconomic divides, where the rich accumulated wealth through deceit and bribery, exacerbating class-based injustices that Amos vehemently opposed.

Alongside socio-economic injustices, Amos reproved the seduction of Israel by idolatrous practices displacing Yahweh's worship. The prophet's particular focus on shrines such as Bethel and Gilgal highlighted where such apostasies visibly transpired. Amos 4:4-5 sarcastically challenges their empty rituals: "Go to Bethel and sin; go to Gilgal and sin yet more... Burn leavened bread as a thank offering and brag about your freewill offerings—boast about them, you Israelites, for this is what you love to do," (NIV) implying that these religious acts, devoid of genuine devotion and ethical conduct, are profane caricatures of true worship.

Idolatry, in Amos's theology, was not merely religious infidelity; it was an ethical bankruptcy. By engaging in sycophantic reverence for foreign deities and corrupted worship practices, Israelites turned a blind eye to justice and righteousness, thus failing to emulate divine principles. The polarizing effect of idolatry cultivated a society blind to its covenantal responsibilities, making Amos's message of returning to sincere worship and justice crucial for national redemption.

Amos thus emerges not merely as a historical figure but as a timeless advocate for social justice, parity, and authentic devotion—an eloquent reminder that societal ethics are inherently tethered to the spiritual fervor and fidelity to God's covenantal precepts. His prophecies resonate even today, providing a template for scrutinizing our institutions' ethical fabric against the immutable standards of justice and divine righteousness.

In sum, Amos's indictment of Israel's transgressions underscores a profound theological commitment to understanding that worship of God cannot exist in a vacuum devoid of justice. This seamless binding of faith and ethics sets the book apart in the canon, urging both ancient and modern audiences to embrace a holistic covenantal relationship reflective in equitable, just living.

The Visions of Amos: Locusts, Fire, and the Plumb Line

The book of Amos captivates its readers with a series of vivid visions that illuminate the consequences of Israel's continuous defiance against divine commandments. The three visions of locusts, fire, and the plumb line, serve as both symbolic and explicit warnings, each layered with profound moral and theological significances.

1. The Vision of Locusts

Amos commences with the vision of locusts in Amos 7:1-3, portraying a prophetic scene that is as striking as it is alarming: "This is what the Sovereign Lord showed me: He was preparing swarms of locusts after the king's share had been harvested and just as the late crops were coming up." This vision encapsulates agricultural devastation, a scenario Israelites would fear immensely due to their dependence on agriculture.

The locusts, symbolic agents of divine wrath, are set to strip the land bare, threatening the nation's survival. Commentators like Anderson and Freedman suggest that this is a metaphor for the impending Assyrian invasion (Anderson, G.W., Freedman, D.N., The Anchor Yale Bible Dictionary, 1992). The fact that Amos intercedes, pleading, "Sovereign Lord, forgive! How can Jacob survive? He is so small!" (Amos 7:2), and that the Lord relents, reflects the potential for repentance and divine mercy—an essential theme in Amos's prophecies.

2. The Vision of Fire

The second vision involves fire: "This is what the Lord showed me: The Lord was calling for judgment by fire; it dried up the great deep and devoured the land" (Amos 7:4). Fire here is a potent symbol of judgment, indicative of total destruction. This divine fire, unlike the locusts, is more encompassing, suggesting a more severe form of punishment that affects both land and sea—the "great deep."

As Paul L. Redditt explains in "Introduction to the Prophets" (Redditt, P.L., 2008), the fire vision emphasizes an intensification of the threat level due to Israel's continued disobedience. The rhetorical element of escalation indicates a narrowing window for repentance. Once more, Amos's pleading has an effect: "Then I cried out, 'Sovereign Lord, I beg you, stop! How can Jacob survive? He is so small!' So the Lord relented" (Amos 7:5-6), showcasing divine patience amidst mounting judgment.

3. The Vision of the Plumb Line

The third, and arguably the most intricate vision, is that of the plumb line: "This is what he showed me: The Lord was standing by a wall that had been built true to plumb, with a plumb line in his hand" (Amos 7:7). The plumb line, as highlighted by S.D. Snyman in "The Socio-Historical Context of the Book of Amos" (Snyman, S.D., 2006), serves as a metaphor for divine standards of justice and righteousness against which Israel is measured.

This vision lacks the mediatory aspect of the previous two, indicating a shift toward unavoidable judgment: "The Lord said, 'Look, I am setting a plumb line among my people Israel; I will spare them no longer'" (Amos 7:8). It marks a culmination in Amos's message—a pivot from warnings that allow for mercy, to judgment that consummates divine justice. The plumb line thus represents an ultimate diagnostic of Israel's societal and spiritual crookedness, a verdict of inevitable divine action rather than a threat of it.

Conclusion

The visions of Amos underscore the gravity of Israel's predicament due to its social injustice and idolatry. The narrative progression from locusts to fire to the plumb line illustrates a narrowing of grace, transitioning from possible repentance to conclusive judgment. Each vision opens a window into the heart of God's justice—patient yet resolute. As J.A. Motyer notes in "The Message of Amos" (Motyer, J.A., 1974), these visions act as a moral compass for readers, challenging us to introspect our own moral and ethical alignments in view of divine justice.

These vividly portrayed visions remain relevant, compelling us to consider the implications in today's context and inviting readers to reflect on the conditions of their societies and the quality of their justice systems against God's unwavering standards.

The Rejection of Amos's Warnings: Response from Bethel

In the unfolding drama of the prophetic ministry of Amos, one of the most poignant episodes takes place in Bethel, a major religious and political center under the northern kingdom of Israel. Bethel, whose name translates to "House of God," was not only home to one of the principal sanctuaries, established as a royal shrine under King Jeroboam I, but it also symbolized the heart of Israel's spiritual confusion, where the worship of Yahweh was entwined with pagan rituals. This chapter examines the rejection and resistance Amos encountered as he delivered God's warnings, focusing on the response from Bethel.

Amos's prophetic ministry was grounded in the divine calling he received, as described in Amos 7:14-15, where he asserts, "I was neither a prophet nor the son of a prophet, but I was a shepherd, and I also took care of sycamore-fig trees. But the LORD took me from tending the flock and said to me, 'Go, prophesy to my people Israel.'" (NIV). His message was clear and uncompromising: Israel's prosperity had led to complacency, spiritual corruption, and social injustice, which would incur divine judgment.

First and foremost in understanding the rejection from Bethel is recognizing the status quo Amos was challenging. Bethel represented the established religious orthodoxy endorsed by the state. King Jeroboam II's reign (c. 786–746

BCE) was marked by significant economic growth and territorial expansion, comparable to the prosperous era of Solomon. However, this prosperity was unevenly distributed, fostering rampant social inequalities, exactly what Amos sought to target in his prophecies, as seen in Amos 6:4-6 where he condemns the self-indulgent lifestyles of the rich and powerful.

It was in this atmosphere that Amos confronted Amaziah, the priest of Bethel. In one of the most telling encounters, Amaziah responds to Amos's prophecies with hostility and disdain: "Get out, you seer!" Amaziah orders Amos, deriding his messages as unwelcome interference, "Go back to the land of Judah. Earn your bread there and do your prophesying there." (Amos 7:12, NIV). This account signifies the institutional rejection of Amos's warnings, underscoring a broader refusal to acknowledge the depth of Israel's betrayals against its covenant with God.

By analyzing this reaction, we uncover a deeper layer of resistance that characterizes much of the interaction between prophets and the institutional powers of their time. Amos's outsider status—originating from the southern kingdom of Judah—further emphasized the threat he posed to Bethel's authority and the northern kingdom's complacency. The economic elite of Israel, benefiting from systemic injustices, naturally regarded Amos's calls for justice and righteousness as destabilizing.

Theological scholars often interpret this rejection in prophetic literature as a testimony to the potential dangers faced by those who dare to speak divine truth against societal hypocrisy and moral corruption. This rejection narrative is symbolic of the broader conflict between prophetic truth and entrenched power dynamics. Amos's courageous stand at Bethel is emblematic of a timeless struggle, one that resonates with later prophets such as Jeremiah and even extends into New Testament accounts.

Given Bethel's importance and the vehement rejection Amos faced there, the response from Bethel serves as a critical example of how prophetic messages are received when they challenge power structures and societal norms. Amos's denunciation of the lavish, indulgent lifestyle, supported by systemic injustices, is a rebuke not just against Israel but a universal call for moral introspection and social equity.

Thus, the rejection from Bethel is not merely a historical footnote but an integral reflection on the resistance inherent within human societies to prophetic calls for change. It is a vivid illustration of the prophet's role as both a messenger and a moral arbiter, challenging nations to rise above affluence-driven arrogance and injustice towards a path of righteousness and obedience to God's covenant. In reflecting on these dynamics, modern readers are invited to consider contemporary parallels and the continued relevance of Amos's message within today's sociopolitical contexts.

The Day of the Lord: Impending Doom and Hope

In the biblical narrative, the phrase "The Day of the Lord" emerges as a central theme permeating the prophecies of Amos, resonating with notions of impending doom intertwined with a glimmer of hope. This notion, profound and multifaceted, captures the dual nature of divine intervention - as an occasion of judgment upon the sinful and oppressive, as well as a source of vindication for the righteous and oppressed. Amos, through his graphic depictions, presents a profound warning that is both a threat and a promise, encapsulating the complex relationship between God and His people.

Amos lived during a time of apparent prosperity in the Northern Kingdom of Israel, yet beneath the surface lay a society riddled with injustice, idolatry, and moral decay. The prophet Amos, although not of noble birth and originally a shepherd from Tekoa, was called to confront the societal ills and spiritual apostasy of Israel (Amos 7:14-15). He utilized the concept of "The Day of the Lord" to jolt the complacent nation into an awareness of its impending downfall.

Amos's depiction of "The Day of the Lord" is vividly alarming: "Woe to you who desire the day of the Lord! Why would you have the day of the Lord? It is darkness, and not light" (Amos 5:18, ESV). Here, Amos warns against a misguided yearning for divine intervention. Rather than a jubilant celebration of deliverance, the Day would unveil divine judgment against those who perpetuate injustice, irrespective of their covenant identity. He portrays it as a day of darkness and calamity, a stark reminder that God's expectation of righteousness transcends mere ritualistic observance.

Moreover, the prophet critiques the superficial religiosity prevalent among the Israelites. The stark pronouncement against their hollow worship - "I hate, I despise your feasts, and I take no delight in your solemn assemblies" (Amos 5:21, ESV) - underscores the incompatibility of their sacrificial rites with the pervasive social injustices and idolatry that persisted. Through these stark declarations, Amos communicates the futility of rituals devoid of ethical integrity and justice; the Day of the Lord will unveil this hypocrisy with formidable clarity.

Amos's articulation of "The Day of the Lord" is not solely an ominous proclamation of doom but also bears a promise of hope and restoration. This hope, however, is contingent upon repentance and reformation. "Seek good, and not evil, that you may live; and so the Lord, the God of hosts, will be with you, as you have said" (Amos 5:14, ESV). Here lies a bridge to redemption; the people are urged towards actionable contrition and righteousness, embodying God's call for justice and equality.

The concept bears eschatological significance, transcending the immediate historical context of 8th century BCE

Israel, as it foreshadows the eventual establishment of divine justice. Biblical scholars such as R. Sinclair and J. D. Watts emphasize this duality as critical to understanding Amos's theology of judgment and hope (Sinclair, 1993; Watts, 2002). Amos establishes a framework where God's justice prevails as both punitive and redemptive, reflecting divine compassion for the downtrodden and repentance-driven possibility for spiritual renewal.

In conclusion, "The Day of the Lord" epitomizes the dual potential of destruction and redemption pervasive in the Book of Amos. By invoking this formidable day, Amos implores his audience to realign with God's will - a call that remains strikingly relevant as it echoes through the annals of history into contemporary theological discourse. As the concept unfurls through these prophecies, it serves as a potent academic and spiritual point of exploration, unraveling the immutable connection between divine judgment, justice, and hope.

The teachings and warnings encapsulated in "The Day of the Lord" thereby emphasize the immutable necessity for justice and righteousness, perennially underscoring the theological and ethical mandates that resonate with timeless vigour. Embedded within the narrative's nuances is a profound exhortation for transformation, transcending its historical foothold to impact believers across successive generations, offering both a caution and a beacon for divine and ethical alignment.

Themes of Justice and Righteousness in Amos's Teachings

The themes of justice and righteousness are central to the teachings of Amos, a prophet who emerged from the southern kingdom of Judah to deliver God's message to the northern kingdom of Israel during a time of economic prosperity and social injustice. Understanding these themes is crucial not only to comprehending Amos's prophecies but also to appreciating their profound relevance in both biblical and contemporary contexts.

Amos's era was characterized by a significant socio-economic divide. The wealthy elites of Israel enjoyed a life of opulence while the poor suffered exploitation and deprivation. According to Amos, such a societal structure was anathema to the covenantal ethics that Israel was supposed to uphold. Justice ('mishpat') and righteousness ('tsedaqah') form the backbone of Amos's prophetic critique. His messages convey that these concepts are not merely legalistic requirements but deeply moral principles intrinsic to the character of God and the expectation for those who claim to follow Him.

In the book of Amos, the theme of justice is prominently highlighted through vivid imagery and direct pronouncements. Amos decries the corruption of justice in Israel's courts, where the wealthy could bribe judges at the expense of the poor: "For I know how many are your transgressions and how great are your sins—you who afflict the just, who take a bribe, and turn aside the needy in the gate" (Amos 5:12, New Revised Standard Version). This indictment underscores a societal framework where the very institutions meant to protect the vulnerable instead participated in their oppression. Justice, for Amos, is not merely retributive but restorative, aiming to restore society to a state of fairness where all individuals have their due.

Righteousness, on the other hand, is portrayed as the continual right living that aligns with God's will. Amos calls for a return to genuine piety, devoid of empty ritualism. He communicates God's disdain for insincere worship that divorces itself from ethical living: "I hate, I despise your festivals, and I take no delight in your solemn assemblies... But let justice roll down like waters, and righteousness like an ever-flowing stream" (Amos 5:21, 24). This passage strikingly juxtaposes hollow religious ceremonies with the divine ideal of justice and righteousness, calling Israel to repentance and action.

The prophetic call for justice and righteousness in Amos is not merely a critique of legal and religious practices but also a profound theological assertion about God's nature. God is depicted as a deity of justice who demands that His people reflect this aspect of His character in their social interactions and community structures. Amos's messages present an unyielding insight into the divine expectation for ethical congruence between belief and behavior, critiquing any form of compartmentalization where worship and daily life are seen as separate.

A significant part of Amos's emphasis on justice and righteousness is his vision of an equitable social order. The people of Israel are reminded of their historical role as a chosen nation meant to embody God's laws and reflect His character to the world. However, their failure to uphold justice made them liable to the same standards of judgment they levied upon their neighboring nations. Amos thus warns that privilege brings with it the responsibility to uphold justice and righteousness, failing which they would face the inevitable consequences of divine judgment.

As modern readers engage with the book of Amos, the enduring themes of justice and righteousness resonate strikingly with contemporary issues of social inequality and ethical leadership. The critique of systemic injustice, the call for integrity, and the insistence on genuine worship challenge current societal norms and call individuals and communities to self-examination and reform. In this light, Amos serves as both a historical and prophetic voice, urging structures of power to align with divine principles of equity and ethical consistency.

By dissecting the themes of justice and righteousness within Amos's teachings, we gain insights not only into the ancient social fabric of Israel but also into the continuing relevance and urgency of these issues today. The book of Amos thus transcends its historical context, providing timeless guidance and a prophetic challenge to pursue justice and live righteously in a world that frequently falls short of these divine ideals.

Theological Implications: Amos's Vision of God and Justice

In the book of Amos, one of the most striking elements is the theological portrait it presents. Amos's vision of God is not merely as a distant deity but as an intimately involved moral force demanding justice and righteousness. This distinction offers profound implications for both the ancient audience and modern readers. Amos, although a prophet of doom, presents a vision of divine justice that transcends mere judgment, focusing on ethical requirements and the necessity of societal correction.

Amos's preaching occurred during a time of relative prosperity in Israel under King Jeroboam II (circa 782-753 BCE). Despite economic and political stability, there was a significant moral and spiritual decline, characterized by social injustice and idolatry. Amos's ministry aimed to challenge these societal issues by presenting a theology where morality is deeply enshrined in divine commands. As Amos firmly establishes, God does not overlook transgression and injustice, irrespective of ritualistic faithfulness. This theological stance is echoed in Amos 5:21-24, where he declares: "I despise your religious festivals; your assemblies are a stench to me...But let justice roll on like a river, righteousness like a never-failing stream!"

At the core of Amos's theological implications is the portrayal of God as a ruler who demands ethical social conduct. The contrasts within Amos's messages are stark; they oppose societal norms that prioritize wealth and ceremonial observance over justice and righteousness. Just as the prophet confronted corruption and oppression among Israel's leaders, his messages underscore God's expectation for humans to act equitably. This is articulated in Amos 3:2 where God states, "You only have I chosen of all the families of the earth; therefore I will punish you for all your sins," emphasizing Israel's covenant responsibility to uphold justice as a chosen nation.

Central to Amos's vision is the interrelation of justice and righteousness, concepts that represent divine standards for human behavior. Within the Hebrew context, 'justice' ('mishpat') refers to that which is legally and morally right, while 'righteousness' ('tsedeqah') extends beyond legal conformity to include societal norms. This dual concept is pivotal in Amos's call for a society that manifests God's character through equitable and fair treatment of its members, portraying a vision that acknowledges God's sovereignty over moral law.

The imagery used by Amos further illustrates the theological premise where divine justice is aesthetically present in human affairs. The visions of locusts, fire, and the plumb line are particularly revealing. The plumb line (Amos 7:7-8) symbolizes God's standard of righteousness, against which Israel is measured and found wanting. Such imagery communicates that divine judgment is not arbitrary but is a natural consequence of failing to adhere to God's ethical standards.

However, it is crucial to recognize that Amos's theological implications are not solely focused on divine judgment. Interwoven in his declarations of impending doom is the possibility of hope and restoration. Amos 9:11-15 presents a vision of restoration—a remnant of hope that underscores God's desire for repentance and renewal. Thus, Amos simultaneously warns of judgment and invites his audience into a restored relationship with God, characterized by justice and righteousness.

Beyond the immediate context, the theological implications of Amos resonate through time. Modern interpretations see Amos's teachings as a clarion call for contemporary issues of economic inequality, systemic injustice, and the moral responsibilities of nations and individuals. The timeless questions within Amos speak across history, challenging both ancient and modern societies to reflect divine justice in their laws and communal relations.

In essence, Amos's vision of God as an advocate for justice and ethical behavior challenges believers to re-examine the dynamics of piety and social responsibility. By portraying God as deeply invested in societal justice, Amos establishes a theological framework that elevates the role of ethical action within the life of faith—such a framework remains crucial in the ongoing quest for global justice and equity today.

Modern Interpretations and Relevance: Amos's Message Today

As we grapple with the timeless words of the prophet Amos, we find a message that resonates profoundly with contemporary society. Amos's declarations of judgment are not mere relics of an ancient past; they provide an enduring critique that holds relevance in addressing modern social, economic, and moral dilemmas. This perspective invites us to explore Amos's prophecies through the lens of today's world, examining how his ancient oracles speak to our current circumstances and moral imperatives.

Amos's primary concern was the ethical and social failures of his time, particularly the disparities between the rich and the poor, as well as the widespread injustices perpetuated against vulnerable populations. Today's world, with its stark economic inequalities and systemic injustices, mirrors some of the core issues Amos confronted. The prophet's clarion call for justice, encapsulated in his famous declaration, "But let justice roll on like a river, righteousness like a never-failing stream!" (Amos 5:24, NIV), serves as a timeless exhortation for modern societies striving toward equity and justice.

The pertinence of Amos's message is further underscored by the prophetic denunciation of idolatry and materialism. In an age characterized by consumerism and material excess, Amos challenges contemporary believers to evaluate where their true devotion lies. The prophet condemns the superficial worship practices of his time, emphasizing the futility of ritual without righteousness. His words compel a modern audience to assess the sincerity and depth of their spiritual commitments amid a culture prone to hollow displays of religiosity.

Furthermore, Amos's message has significant implications for social justice advocacy today. Rooted in his prophetic insistence on justice and righteousness, modern readers are called to be active participants in combating inequalities and defending the rights of the marginalized. The prophet's charges against Israel for their social injustices resonate with current issues such as economic exploitation, racial discrimination, and gender inequities. Thus, Amos provides a theological framework for engaging in social activism, reminding believers that their faith is inherently tied to their pursuit of justice.

In addition to social justice, the ecological undertones of Amos's visions, such as the locusts and fire (Amos 7:1-4), offer a pertinent reflection on humanity's relationship with the environment. In an era where environmental concerns are increasingly urgent, Amos's imagery invites a dialogue on sustainable practices and the ethical stewardship of creation. As the prophet warned against the consequences of neglect and destruction, his message serves as a foundational text for advocating ecological responsibility and sustainable development.

Modern scholarship also points to Amos's depiction of the "Day of the Lord" (Amos 5:18-20) as having enduring theological relevance. This concept speaks to the imminent accountability and divine justice that transcends temporal contexts. For contemporary Christians, it underscores the necessity of living with an awareness of divine accountability, urging a life marked by vigilance, ethical integrity, and eschatological hope.

As we synthesize Amos's prophetic utterances with today's challenges, his teachings beckon a transformative response. For religious communities, the message calls for profound introspection and meaningful action in embodying the principles of justice, mercy, and humility before God. Amos's prophetic voice ultimately serves as both a challenge and an inspiration, urging individuals and societies toward a just and faithful engagement with the world.

In conclusion, the book of Amos remains a seminal text that speaks with urgency and relevance to the moral and social issues of our day. By revisiting Amos's pronouncements through the lens of modern realities, we not only preserve the prophet's enduring legacy, but also continue to derive guiding principles for faithful living in a complex and often unjust world. Through the prism of Amos's ancient wisdom, believers are called to embody justice and righteousness, extending the transformative power of the prophetic tradition into the present and future.

The modern interpretation of Amos is an invitation to remain vigilant and committed in the face of pervasive challenges, demonstrating that the prophetic message is not confined to its historical context but rather reverberates across time to inspire and convict each generation anew.

Social Justice and Moral Teachings in Amos

Historical Context and Background of Amos' Prophecies

The Book of Amos stands as a profound testament to the intersection of faith and social responsibility in the Hebrew Bible. To fully appreciate the prophetic messages conveyed by Amos, it is crucial to delve into the historical backdrop against which these prophecies were articulated. By understanding the sociopolitical and religious context of Amos' time, we can better grasp the enduring significance of his teachings on social justice and ethics.

Amos, one of the earliest Hebrew prophets, delivered his messages during the reigns of Uzziah in Judah and Jeroboam II in Israel, around the 8th century BCE. This was a period characterized by unprecedented territorial expansion and economic prosperity for the Northern Kingdom of Israel. Archaeological findings and historical records support the notion that the region enjoyed affluence, with trading networks spanning from Damascus to the Nile Valley. This prosperity, however, was not evenly distributed among the people, leading to a stark division between the wealthy elite and the impoverished populace.

The societal structure of Israel during Amos' lifetime was marked by significant disparities in wealth and power. The accumulation of wealth by the elite, often at the expense of the poor, resulted in social and economic stratification. Landownership played a pivotal role, with large estates owned by a few, while many lived as tenant farmers or laborers. This concentration of wealth contributed to systemic injustices, including corruption in legal systems and exploitation of the marginalized—a stark contradiction to the covenantal laws that emphasized justice and care for the vulnerable.

Religiously, the Israelites maintained a robust temple culture centered in Bethel and other high places, which they believed secured divine favor. However, as Amos confronted them, this religious observance was superficial and devoid of genuine moral adherence. As noted by scholars, "Amos' indictments highlight the dissonance between ritualistic worship and moral conduct, demonstrating God's demand for justice and righteousness over mere ceremonial observances."

The political climate of the era also influenced Amos' prophecies. Israel's alliances and military campaigns brought about a deceptive sense of security, yet these were accompanied by increasing oppression and societal decay. The strategic positioning of Israel within the ancient Near East both enriched and imperiled the nation. Economic treaties bolstered wealth yet fostered an environment where social inequities thrived, and the voices of the oppressed were silenced.

Against this backdrop, Amos emerged not from the priestly or royal elite but from the humble profession of shepherding and fig-tending in Tekoa, a town in Judah. His outsider status perhaps afforded him a unique perspective on the entrenched injustices within Israel. As Amos' call to prophecy insists, his mission was divinely ordained, "The Lord took me from following the flock, and the Lord said to me, 'Go, prophesy to my people Israel'" (Amos 7:15).

In summary, understanding the historical context of Amos' prophecies reveals a society at the crossroads of economic abundance and moral bankruptcy. It underscores a divine insistence on justice and righteousness that transcends millennia. By examining the dynamics of Amos' time, we gain insights into the perennial challenges of aligning faith and social ethics—a task as relevant today as it was in the prophet's era.

This historical background sets the stage for exploring the thematic core of Amos' teachings, where justice and righteousness not only define societal ideals but serve as a divine mandate for moral living across generations.

The Central Themes of Justice and Righteousness in Amos

In exploring the central themes of justice and righteousness in the Book of Amos, one uncovers profound insights into the moral and ethical expectations that the prophet Amos communicated to the people of Israel. The overriding concern with justice and righteousness establishes Amos as a pivotal figure advocating for social reform and divine accountability within the Hebrew Bible.

Amos's prophecies articulate a vision where justice ('mishpat') and righteousness ('tsedaqah') serve as the foundation of a society that aligns with God's intentions. These twin themes permeate the narrative, weaving a complex tapestry that challenges the societal norms and behaviors of ancient Israel. It is through this lens that Amos delivers his most poignant critiques, becoming a voice for the undeniably oppressed and marginalized. This emphasis is captured in Amos 5:24: "But let justice roll on like a river, righteousness like a never-failing stream" (NIV). This imagery of flowing, cleansing water symbolically portrays justice and righteousness as unending forces of divine will, calling for continuous moral rectitude.

The historical backdrop of Amos' writings provides crucial context for understanding these themes. During a period of relative prosperity under the reigns of Jeroboam II in Israel and Uzziah in Judah, economic affluence resulted in social stratification, corruption, and complacency among the wealthy elite. While the upper class luxuriated in their wealth, the poor were exploited and disenfranchised, leading to systemic injustices that Amos directly addresses.

Justice in the context of Amos is multifaceted, pertaining not merely to legal rectitude but encompassing social equity and fairness. According to Robert Carroll, a noted biblical scholar, Amos critiques the legal systems in Israel, which favored the affluent and powerful, stating: "there are those who turn justice to bitterness and cast righteousness to the ground" (Amos 5:7, NIV). Carroll's analysis reveals that Amos's call to justice is a demand for the redistribution of power and privilege, an eradication of deceitful practices that have sullied the covenantal relationship between Israel and God.

Righteousness, on the other hand, is deeply rooted in ethical conduct based on covenantal laws and agreements. It is concerned with the individual's alignment with God's moral statutes. For Amos, righteousness does not exist in a vacuum but is inseparably linked with justice; an individual's actions should reflect a broader commitment to societal welfare. As Gerhard von Rad explicates, righteousness in Amos is not solely personal piety but "conduct that harmonizes with God's ethical demands, resulting in balanced and fair community interactions."

Amos places profound emphasis on moral integrity, as denoted in his denouncement of religious hypocrisy. Despite Israel's participation in temple rituals and festivals, their neglect of social responsibilities invalidated these religious acts. "I hate, I despise your religious festivals; your assemblies are a stench to me" (Amos 5:21, NIV). This stern pronouncement underscores Amos's belief that genuine worship is inseparable from social justice and ethical behavior, an idea that Thomas L. Leclerc notes in his critique of ancient Israel's religious practices.

Furthermore, Leonard K. Singer explores how Amos uniquely prioritizes justice over sacrificial offerings, indicating a theological shift where moral actions outweigh liturgical practices. Singer posits that Amos's focus is on transformative action, urging society to embody divine justice as a testimony of faith.

The central themes of justice and righteousness in Amos extend beyond mere condemnation; they include hope for repentance and redemption. Amos's prophecies envisage a society that can reorient itself according to divine principles, transforming into a community characterized by equity and empathy. Justice, in this sense, becomes a divine imperative for national survival and a reflection of God's own righteous nature.

In conclusion, Amos confronts both the individuals and the nation's systemic structures with a prophetic call that reverberates through time, shaping not only the spiritual consciousness of ancient Israel but also modern interpretations of ethical and social justice frameworks. The enduring power of Amos's message lies in its ability to challenge contemporary social structures, encouraging a continuous pursuit of justice and righteousness as enduring components of a faithful and equitable society. Scholars like Walter Brueggemann have emphasized this dynamic relationship, asserting that Amos's prophecy remains "an urgent call to assess collective moral health and align with God's just purposes for humanity."

The Denunciation of Social Injustice and Oppression

The Book of Amos, a prophetic text from the Old Testament, serves as a poignant voice against social injustice and oppression that was prevalent in the Northern Kingdom of Israel during the 8th century BCE. This denunciation is not only central to the prophetic message delivered by Amos but also forms a critical theological and ethical discourse that resonates with readers through the ages. This section seeks to analyze and interpret Amos' fierce criticism of social inequities and the moral underpinnings of his proclamations.

Amos' background as a herdsman and a dresser of sycamore-fig trees is significant in understanding his perspective on social justice. Unencumbered by affiliations with the monarchy or priesthood, Amos spoke from a position of relative independence and authenticity. His outsider status allowed him to deliver his messages without the potential biases that might affect those within the societal upper echelons—a stance that granted him both clarity and a piercing directness in his criticism of those in power.

In his oracles, Amos targets the societal elite and those who benefit from economic and social structures that marginalize the poor and vulnerable. His denunciations are visceral and unyielding, as evident in his declaration: "They sell the righteous for silver, and the needy for a pair of sandals" (Amos 2:6, NRSV). This accusation underscores the commodification of human life and the prioritization of material gain over ethical conduct. The prophet's message challenges unjust practices by exposing the moral bankruptcy inherent within Israel's socioeconomic policies and the leadership's penchant for avarice and unfair advantage.

Amos' rhetoric intensifies as he condemns the corruption permeating the justice system: "For I know how many are your transgressions, and how great are your sins—you who afflict the righteous, who take a bribe, and push aside the needy in the gate" (Amos 5:12, NRSV). The 'gate' refers to the place of legal proceedings, suggesting that the very institutions meant to protect and ensure justice were themselves complicit in perpetuating inequality. Amos reminds his audience that societal health is contingent upon justice and righteousness, principles that must be upheld to align the community with divine expectations.

Amos not only censures corrupt practices but also calls for a societal restructuring that embodies justice: "But let justice roll down like waters, and righteousness like an ever-flowing stream" (Amos 5:24, NRSV). The imagery employed here is powerful and evocative, suggesting a relentless and life-giving flow of justice that has the transformative potential to reshape society. The metaphor of justice as a vital and sustaining force is both inspiring and challenging, urging the community to integrate justice into the very fabric of their existence.

Furthermore, Amos equates social injustice with religious hypocrisy, reprimanding those who engage in elaborate religious rituals while neglecting ethical conduct: "I hate, I despise your festivals, and I take no delight in your solemn assemblies" (Amos 5:21, NRSV). This denunciation highlights a disconnect between ritualistic worship and true moral behavior, asserting that divine favor does not overlook social transgressions. Amos presents a compelling argument for the indivisibility of ethical and spiritual life, championing a lived faith that embraces mercy and justice as central tenets.

In conclusion, the Book of Amos presents a robust critique of societal inequality and challenges readers to confront issues of injustice with unwavering moral conviction. Amos' denunciation of social injustices is not merely a historical account but a didactic narrative that calls for introspection and action in striving towards equitable societies. As a prophetic voice, his message continues to echo across centuries, compelling adherents and scholars alike to grapple with the imperatives of justice and righteousness in their own contexts.

Economic Inequality and Exploitation in Israelite Society

The socio-economic landscape of Israelite society during the time of Amos was characterized by significant disparities and an emerging class divide that prompted his poignant denunciations. As an acute observer of social conditions, Amos critiqued the stark contrast between the opulence of the few and the destitution of the many. In his prophetic ministry, Amos highlighted the exploitation and systemic injustices that permeated the economic infrastructure of his time.

Amos operated in an era when Israel, particularly under King Jeroboam II, experienced unprecedented prosperity, largely due to success in commerce and expansionist policies. However, this wealth was concentrated in the hands of a small elite, while a significant portion of society languished in poverty. The prophet castigated the affluent for their luxurious lifestyles, as evidenced by phrases such as "they drink wine in bowls and anoint themselves with the finest oils" (Amos 6:6), illustrating their indulgence and ignorance towards the suffering around them.

Economic inequality in ancient Israel was exacerbated by an agrarian economy that favored landowners and merchants, who held power both economically and politically. This system enabled and perpetuated the disenfranchisement of the lower classes, chiefly farmers and laborers. Amos vehemently condemned practices such as the unjust acquisition of land and the exploitation of laborers, encapsulated in his statement, "because you trample on the poor and take from him levies of grain" (Amos 5:11). Such acts were not isolated, as the judicial system, too, was fraught with corruption and bias, often pandering to the interests of the wealthy at the expense of the needy.

Moreover, debt slavery, a common practice at the time, is singled out by Amos as a particular form of exploitation. In a society that relied on annual harvests, any failure in crops could lead to debt, which farmers often couldn't repay without losing their land or even their freedom. "They sell the righteous for silver, and the needy for a pair of sandals" (Amos 2:6) serves as a powerful critique of how financial dominance translated into social power, further deepening the socio-economic divide. This imagery of selling humans trivializes the value of life, reducing individuals to mere commodities within an unbalanced system.

The prophetic literature of Amos not only unveiled these economic injustices but also acted as an indictment of moral failure and societal collapse. Amos implored Israel to uphold justice and righteousness, urging the nation to "hate evil, and love good, and establish justice in the gate" (Amos 5:15). Implicit in this plea was the understanding that the divine prosperity envisioned for Israel was unattainable without equitable social structures.

While Amos's prophecies were contextually rooted in his contemporary Israel, they offer enduring lessons on economic justice. His critical perspective challenges modern readers to reflect on how wealth and power dynamics continue to resonate within contemporary societies, urging a reevaluation of economic systems through a moral and ethical lens steeped in justice and compassion.

Moral and Ethical Teachings Within Amos' Warnings

The Book of Amos, rich in its prophetic declarations and timeless implications, ventures deeply into issues of morality and ethics through its dire warnings to Israel. As a shepherd turned prophet, Amos passionately delivers messages that not only critique the socio-political climate of his time but also resonate profoundly with universal ethical principles. This section explores Amos' powerful integration of moral imperatives within his warnings, inviting introspection on the essence of justice and righteousness as vital components of societal integrity.

Amos addresses a society entrenched in opulence and idolatrous practices, contrasting sharply with its evident neglect for the vulnerable and an outright dismissal of divine commands. Within his prophecies, Amos repeatedly emphasizes the interconnectedness of ethical behavior and worship. This concept is starkly exemplified in the condemnation of empty rituals devoid of moral rectitude. In Amos 5:22-24, he delivers a potent critique of religious ceremonies, declaring: "Even though you bring me burnt offerings and grain offerings, I will not accept them...But let justice roll on like a river, righteousness like a never-failing stream!" This famous passage underscores that authentic devotion to God encompasses genuine commitment to justice and ethical integrity, not merely external observances.

The moral teachings interwoven within Amos' warnings are not limited to general exhortations of justice but extend to explicit denouncements of specific societal sins. These include the oppression of the poor, deceit, and corruption among the wealthy and powerful. In Amos 2:6-7, the prophet depicts the unchecked injustices within Israel: "They sell the innocent for silver, and the needy for a pair of sandals. They trample on the heads of the poor as on the dust of the ground and deny justice to the oppressed." Here, Amos denounces the commodification of human lives and the drastic consequences of economic manipulation. This passage unveils a stark moral decline in which the value of life is trivialized for material gain—a violation of divine justice and an affront to the ethical foundations of a godly society.

Amos also fiercely criticizes the duplicity and materialism pervasive among Israel's elites, lambasting their complacency and indulgence at the expense of ethical living. Through vivid portrayals and rhetorical questions in Amos 6:4-6, he exposes their luxurious lifestyles: "You lie on beds adorned with ivory and lounge on your couches... but you do not grieve over the ruin of Joseph." This critique is not a mere denunciation of wealth but an ethical appeal against the moral numbness and detachment from communal suffering. Amos' warnings implore the affluent to transcend their self-indulgence, advocating for empathy, gratitude, and shared responsibility.

The moral fabric of Amos' teachings is woven with exhortations toward repentance and reform, suggesting that adherence to ethical principles can avert divine wrath. In Amos 5:14-15, the prophet offers a path toward divine favor, exhorting, "Seek good, not evil, that you may live...Hate evil, love good; maintain justice in the courts." This call for righteous living underscores a transformative vision wherein ethical conduct aligns with divine will, potentially restoring societal harmony and divine blessings.

Amos' moral and ethical exhortations, although rooted in the context of ancient Israel, possess an enduring universality.

They challenge contemporary societies to reflect on their ethical standards and inspire a collective moral consciousness. The prophet's emphasis on justice, equity, and sincere worship continues to echo across centuries, urging present generations to infuse ethical behavior within personal and communal realms. Ultimately, Amos' warnings serve as a timeless ethical compass, prompting societies to attain not only material prosperity but moral excellence and divine favor.

The Role of the Prophets in Upholding Social Justice

In the tapestry of biblical narrative, prophets serve an indelible role as the voice of divine will, bridging the ethereal chasm between God and humanity. The Book of Amos is no exception, wherein Amos emerges not merely as a harbinger of doom but as a fervent advocate for social justice. His proclamations reflect a profound commitment to addressing the moral and ethical deficit pervasive within Israelite society during his time.

Amos, a herdsman from Tekoa, stands as a paradigmatic figure among the minor prophets, uniquely conscious of the sociopolitical turmoils besetting his contemporaries. The socio-economic landscape during Amos's prophecy was riddled with stark inequalities and exploitation, elements he vehemently opposed. The Book of Amos distinctively elevates social justice as a pinnacle of divine concern—though framed within the broader religious context of His covenant with Israel. Amos's prophetic voice echoes through time, compounding the moral obligation of society to uphold justice as articulated in Amos 5:24: "But let justice roll on like a river, righteousness like a never-failing stream!" (NIV).

Throughout his oracles, Amos consistently calls for the rectification of systemic injustices. Scholars such as Wolff (1983) argue that Amos conceptualized social justice as not merely a political or social agenda, but a divine mandate integral to covenant faithfulness. His prophetic literature is saturated with denunciations of societal malpractices, including idolatry and inequity, positioning justice as a core attribute of divine nature (Wolff, Hans Walter, "Joel and Amos", Fortress Press, 1983).

Amos's prophecies were accessible, transcending the aristocratic echelons to reach the common person. His pronouncements emphasized that the divine expectation for justice was incumbent upon all societal strata, from kings and priests to merchants and farmers. This egalitarian approach is poignantly illustrated in his vivid metaphors and rhetorical questions, crafted not only to admonish but also to elicit a communal awakening to the necessity of moral conduct.

The prophet's role, therefore, was multifarious—comprising elements of social critique, moral instruction, and theological reflection. Amos did not merely articulate divine displeasure; he actively engaged in a form of advocacy that sought to catalyze societal transformation. His messages conveyed the inherent risks of divine judgment attributable to moral laxity and neglect of communal welfare. As scholars like Niehaus (1992) propose, Amos's insistence on justice was inherently tethered to true worship, devoid of ceremonial hypocrisy (Niehaus, Jeffrey J., "Amos", Baker Books, 1992).

Amos's impassioned calls for justice extended beyond rebuke. They also offered insights into the nature and expectation of a covenant relationship with God, where social justice was inherently linked to spiritual fidelity. The prophet's persistence in addressing inequality and oppression reinforced the notion that morality and ethics were inseparable from religious observance.

In examining Amos's influence within the prophetic corpus, one recognizes his pivotal contribution to the ancient discourse on justice. His distinctive voice underscores the continuity and variance in prophetic roles throughout the biblical narrative—each tasked with specific divine mandates but collectively emphasizing justice as indispensable to the human-divine relationship.

The lasting impact of Amos's advocacy remains relevant, inviting contemporary readers to consider the applicability of his messages in modern contexts. The role of the prophet—then and now—is not only to forecast or forewarn but to elucidate and enforce divine principles of justice. This establishes a timeless ideal, urging continuous reflection on how societies can realign their moral compasses to emulate the justice Amos so passionately espoused.

The Consequences of Ignoring Divine Justice

The Book of Amos holds a critical place within the Minor Prophets of the Hebrew Bible, standing out with its persistent call for social justice and an unwavering spotlight on divine justice. Amos, a shepherd and fig grower from Tekoa, was tasked by God to prophesy to the northern kingdom of Israel during a time of pronounced prosperity. This prosperity, however, belied a deep-seated corruption permeating every layer of society. The narrative intertwines a divine mandate for justice with stark warnings about the consequences for ignoring this divine principle.

The systemic inequalities and unchecked injustices evident in Amos's era provoked a divine judgment articulated powerfully through the prophet. Amos's pronouncements were not mere observations but rather an urgent clarion call alerting to the moral decay and spiritual disobedience that had become rampant in Israel. Economic exploitation, judicial corruption, and religious hypocrisy were met not only with divine disapprobation but with an unequivocal pronouncement of impending divine intervention.

Within the prophetic articulations of Amos, the consequences of ignoring divine justice are elucidated with theological profundity and prophetic vehemence. God, depicted as the ultimate arbiter of justice, communicates through Amos a series of calamities that would befall the nation should they continue their neglect of moral and social responsibilities. Amos 3:2 captures the divine prerogative: "You only have I known of all the families of the earth; therefore I will punish you for all your iniquities." This underscores a unique relationship with Israel, implicating them more deeply in their failure to enact justice (The Holy Bible, English Standard Version).

Amos 4:6-11 outlines a series of increasingly severe punishments designed as corrective measures. These include famine, drought, pestilence, and military defeat. Each calamity serves as both a direct consequence of rebellion and a divine invitation to repentance: "I gave you cleanness of teeth in all your cities, and lack of bread in all your places, yet you did not return to me, declares the Lord" (Amos 4:6, ESV). The cyclical refrain, "yet you have not returned to me," punctuates the text, highlighting Israel's continued obstinacy in the face of clear divine signals.

The narrative culminates in an imagery-laden pronouncement of eschatological judgment, emphasizing the gravity of their spiritual negligence. Amos 5:18-20 condemns the superficial yearning for "the Day of the Lord," a time the Israelites mistakenly perceived as their vindication. Amos refutes this misconception: for those neglecting divine justice, it shall be "as if a man fled from a lion, and a bear met him" (Amos 5:19, ESV), signifying inevitable and inescapable ruin.

Furthermore, Amos 5:24 encapsulates the essence of divine justice with an enduring charge: "But let justice roll down like waters, and righteousness like an ever-flowing stream." Here, Amos posits justice and righteousness as non-negotiable divine imperatives, contrasting starkly against Israel's manifest failings. The text implies a continuous, participatory understanding of justice, appealing both to societal systems and individual morality.

The prophetic warnings reach a climactic condemnation in Amos 8:11-12, foretelling a famine "not a famine of bread, nor a thirst for water, but of hearing the words of the Lord." This severe spiritual crisis serves as the ultimate deprivation, severing the sustenance of divine guidance. As Israel plunged deeper into moral corruption, the absence of prophetic counsel symbolizes a profound spiritual void, resulting in societal disintegration.

Amos's messages conclude with an assured promise of restoration contingent on repentance. In Amos 9:11-15, the vision of renewal weaves through the messianic restoration of the "booth of David," signaling the ultimate triumph of justice and righteousness under divine governance. Here, the text suggests that despite severe warnings, the covenantal hope remains intact, predicated on a sincere return to divine ordinances.

Through the lens of Amos, the imperative of aligning societal practices with divine justice emerges persistently. The prophet's message reveals not only the certainty of divine retribution for ignoring justice but underscores the covenantal promise of restoration for those who seek righteous paths. In an enduring theological truth, Amos unambiguously sets forth the consequences of neglecting divine justice, intertwining the fate of a nation with its moral and ethical adherence to divine commandments.

Amos' Vision of a Just Society

The ancient landscape of the Near East, in the tumultuous period of the 8th century BCE, served as the backdrop for the prophetic messages delivered by Amos, whose profound vision for a just society continues to echo through the corridors of history. The book of Amos unveils a picture of Israelite society marred by pronounced social injustices, amidst which Amos steps forward as a harbinger of divine justice and reform. As we delve into Amos' vision of a just society, we explore the intricate tapestry of his calls for equity, fairness, and the restoration of righteousness, all deeply woven into the socio-political fabric of his time.

The societal structure during Amos' time was one of significant disparity, characterized by a marked divide between the affluent elite and the impoverished common folk. Amos, originating from Tekoa—a modest village in Judah—bore the mantle of a prophet not from the formal schools of prophecy but as a shepherd and dresser of sycamore-fig trees. His background brought an earthy perspective to his vocation, allowing him to keenly observe the stark inequalities festering in Israel (Amos 7:14-15). Through his vivid imagery and impassioned speeches, Amos called attention not only to the societal leaders and their complicity but also to the populace's apathy towards the suffering of their brethren (Amos 5:11-12).

Central to Amos' vision was the pursuit of justice ('mishpat') and righteousness ('tsedaqah')—terms that in biblical Hebrew encapsulate a world of rich meanings, far beyond their mere lexical constructs. These terms embody the divine order and ethical responsibilities incumbent upon humans to ensure societal harmony. Amos famously exhorts, "But let justice roll on like a river, righteousness like a never-failing stream!" (Amos 5:24 NIV). This imagery underscores an ongoing, dynamic force of moral rectitude that should pervade the structural and spiritual facets of society.

Further, Amos' vision rebukes systemic corruption and economic exploitation. His prophecies underscore the exploitation evidenced in skewed trade practices, unjust gain, and adulterated measures, as decried in Amos 8:5-6. Through his denunciations, Amos urges a return to ethical business practices and equitable wealth distribution. These calls resonate with the Deuteronomic code, epitomizing a deep moral imperative towards economic equality, reflecting a divine preference for upliftment over oppression.

Typical of his wider context, Amos diverges from mere proclamations and leans into what scholars argue as a theology of communal ethics. Amos calls for holistic worship that transcends ritualistic formalism. His reproof of religious ceremonies devoid of justice—"I hate, I despise your religious festivals; your assemblies are a stench to me" (Amos 5:21 NIV)—exemplifies a groundbreaking prophetic stance that places moral and social conduct above liturgical adherence.

Additionally, in Amos' oratory lies a profound recognition of collective responsibility. He portrays a society as not merely a collection of individuals but a web of linked destinies wherein each person's welfare affects the entire community. Amos proclaims, "Do two walk together unless they have agreed to do so?" (Amos 3:3 NIV), emphasizing the imperative of mutual accord and shared justice as foundational to societal sustainability.

Amos' vision extends beyond a mere critique, presenting a transformative hope—a restored society wherein fairness reigns, and each being inhabits a sphere of equity. Biblical scholar Walter Brueggemann interprets Amos as not just delivering judgment but also instigating a "counter-imagination," challenging his audience to envision and strive towards a reality imbued with divine justice.

In summation, Amos' vision of a just society is a prescient and enduring blueprint. Far from a relic of ancient times, it remains a relevant and compelling narrative, advocating for justice as the epitome of human endeavors. Its reverberations continue to inspire movements for social justice, challenging modern audiences to embody these ancient truths in contemporary contexts. The book of Amos thus stands as a timeless testament to prophetic courage and divine mandate, calling all to live justly and honor the sacred destinies we collectively share.

This examination of Amos' vision challenges us to reconsider the perennial issues of inequality and social justice. As we embrace the timelessness of his teachings, we find an enduring source of wisdom and inspiration, urging us to create societies that reflect these divine principles of equity and righteousness.

Comparative Analysis: Social Justice in Amos and Other Prophets

The prophetic literature of the Hebrew Bible provides a rich tapestry through which one can explore the multifaceted understanding of social justice. Within this sacred literature, the Book of Amos stands as a profound testament to God's unwavering commitment to justice and righteousness. However, Amos is not alone in these proclamations. A comparative analysis with other prophets, specifically Isaiah, Jeremiah, and Micah, offers a broader perspective on how social justice is articulated and the unique contributions of each prophet to the theological discourse.

The Prophet Amos is particularly noted for his eloquent denunciation of social injustice prevalent in the Northern Kingdom of Israel during the eighth century BCE. His prophetic oracles are characterized by a vehement critique of the disparities between the affluent elite and the marginalized, captured poignantly in phrases such as, "they sell the righteous for silver, and the needy for a pair of sandals" (Amos 2:6). The same commitment to social equity resonates with other prophets, albeit with differing emphases and contexts.

Isaiah, contemporaneous with Amos and also offering counsel to the Southern Kingdom of Judah, amplifies the theme of social justice with a vision of Zion redeemed through justice and righteousness. Isaiah 1:17 exhorts the people to "learn to do good; seek justice, correct oppression; bring justice to the fatherless, plead the widow's cause." Here, as in Amos, the call for justice is not merely punitive but restorative, seeking the welfare of those marginalized by society.

Jeremiah, a later prophet, provides a nuanced understanding by associating justice with covenant fidelity. For Jeremiah, the breaking of the covenant is reflected in social injustices, where leaders fail to heed divine ordinances and safeguard the vulnerable. His poignant message in Jeremiah 22:3, which commands, "Do justice and righteousness, and deliver from the hand of the oppressor him who has been robbed," aligns him with the tradition of Amos, underscoring the inseparable nature of righteousness and communal ethics.

Micah, another prophetic voice, most notably encapsulates the call to social justice in his succinct yet profound directive: "He has told you, O man, what is good; and what does the LORD require of you but to do justice, and to love kindness, and to walk humbly with your God" (Micah 6:8). Micah's articulation marries individual piety with social responsibility, offering a holistic approach to divine requirements that is less explicitly drawn in Amos's direct castigations.

While these prophets share a theological affinity concerning social justice, their approaches differ according to their historical and cultural contexts. Amos tends to employ a more confrontational rhetoric, which can be attributed to the socio-economic conditions of the Northern Kingdom and his outsider status as a prophet from Judah. Isaiah and Jeremiah, being more entrenched in political currents, balance their social critiques with visions of renewal and covenant, anticipating divine intervention in history through a messianic hope.

Moreover, the broader historical backdrop of each prophetic ministry influences their social justice discourses. Amos prophesies during a time of relative peace and prosperity, which exacerbates social divisions and unethical wealth accumulation. In contrast, Jeremiah's messages resonate within a period of political tumult and imminent exile, where social injustice is symptomatic of national infidelity to Yahweh's covenant. This differentiation presents itself in the variance in their emphases—from Amos's stark warning of impending doom to Jeremiah's theme of inevitable judgment intertwined with the hope of restoration.

Despite their contextual differences, these prophetic books collectively argue against the notion that religious ritual alone suffices for covenant fidelity. Amos, in perhaps one of his most scathing critiques, decries empty ritualism with the declaration, "I hate, I despise your feasts, and I take no delight in your solemn assemblies" (Amos 5:21). In drawing parallels, Isaiah similarly critiques hollow religiosity unaccompanied by ethical living (Isaiah 1:11-17).

Their impact is further seen in how they influence later theological thought and praxis, becoming foundational for dual themes of justice and righteousness in second-temple Judaism and subsequently in Christian ethical teaching. The continuity and contrasts found among Amos, Isaiah, Jeremiah, and Micah enrich the biblical canon's portrayal of God's unwavering demand for a society marked by justice and compassion.

This comparative exploration reveals that while the prophets individually contextualize their messages, they collectively affirm a unified vision that transcends the immediate historical dynamics. It is a vision that resonates with an ageless truth: divine justice is integral to human existence, requiring active engagement in the pursuit of a societal structure that reflects God's equitable standards. Amos, with his passionate oracles, remains a pivotal figure whose clarion call continues to echo through the chambers of history, demanding adherence to a higher moral and social standard.

Modern Implications of Amos' Teachings on Social Justice

In the rich tapestry of the prophetic literature of the Old Testament, the Book of Amos stands as a profound testament to the enduring relevance of social justice, a theme that echoes through the ages and resonates deeply in today's world. The prophet Amos articulates a formidable critique against the social injustices of his time, presenting moral imperatives that challenge any society grappling with inequity and ethical decay. As we delve into the modern implications of Amos' teachings on social justice, it is essential to unpack how these ancient admonitions apply to contemporary contexts and serve as a moral compass for addressing today's societal challenges.

One of the most striking elements of Amos' prophecies is his uncompromising denunciation of economic exploitation and the avarice that fueled social stratification in ancient Israel. In Amos 5:11, we find the words, "Therefore, because you impose heavy rent on the poor and exact a tribute of grain from them, though you have built houses of well-hewn stone, yet you will not live in them; you have planted pleasant vineyards, yet you will not drink their wine." This condemnation serves as a timeless rebuke against the commodification of human dignity and the systemic extraction of labor and resources from the marginalized for the benefit of the powerful—a scenario eerily reminiscent of many economic injustices seen globally today.

The central ethos of Amos' message is the indivisibility of justice and righteousness, as highlighted in Amos 5:24: "But let justice roll down like waters and righteousness like an ever-flowing stream." This imagery illustrates the prophetic vision of a society constantly nourished and sustained by the principles of fairness and equity, offering a benchmark for evaluating the effectiveness of modern justice systems. The challenge for contemporary societies remains to implement and expand these principles, creating structures that do more than superficially address injustice but actively dismantle embedded inequities.

Modern implications of Amos' teachings are especially poignant in the context of global social movements advocating for rights and equity. The cries for justice heard in protests against systemic racism, gender inequality, and economic disparity resonate with Amos' impassioned oratory. His emphasis on the intrinsic value and inherent dignity of every individual continues to fuel activism and inform policymaking, inspiring contemporary leaders to strive for systemic reforms that mirror the prophet's call for justice.

Amos' focus on accountability aligns with modern demands for transparency and ethics in leadership. As noted by scholars such as James Luther Mays, Amos' role as a societal watchdog requires communal accountability, holding not only individuals but institutions accountable for moral dereliction (Mays, "Amos: A Commentary"). This aspect of Amos' message—insisting that both leaders and ordinary citizens bear responsibility for perpetuating societal injustice—remains crucial as nations wrestle with corruption and seek to foster inclusive governance.

Furthermore, Amos offers an unwavering lens on religious hypocrisy—criticizing those who maintain religious facades while engaging in unethical practices. His admonition, encapsulated in Amos 5:21-23, challenges religious communities today to reconcile their faith with their actions, urging them to become active agents of justice rather than passive observers. This call to authentic faith that produces tangible societal change resonates profoundly in interfaith dialogues and movements that emphasize social justice as intrinsic to spiritual integrity.

In extending Amos' teachings to contemporary environmental and ecological concerns, we see a prophetic antecedent to modern environmental justice movements. The prophetic call to stewardship of land and resources compels today's societies to consider the ethical dimensions of resource management, climate change policy, and the disproportionate impact of environmental degradation on low-income communities. Amos' advocacy for a symbiosis between humanity and the natural world complements today's ethical frameworks that strive to achieve a just and sustainable balance.

In conclusion, the teachings of Amos continue to offer profound insights and guidance. His prophetic voice challenges societies to engage in profound introspection and reformation, fostering a culture where justice prevails over oppression. Amos' clarion calls for justice reverberate across millennia, urging contemporary societies to heed his warnings and actualize his vision of righteousness. Through the integration of Amos' principles into modern frameworks, societies can move closer to realizing an equitable world that honors humanity's collective responsibility to uphold justice and dignity for all.

The Relevance and Interpretation of Amos Today

Contemporary Readings of Amos

The book of Amos, an ancient prophetic work, has remarkable resonance in contemporary discourse. As we examine current interpretations of Amos, our focus shifts towards understanding how its messages are redefined within modern contexts. Although rooted in a specific historical and cultural setting, its themes transcend time, offering timeless insights into justice, morality, and faith.

One of the primary appeals of Amos lies in its bold critique of social injustice. The prophet Amos, speaking in the eighth century BCE, directs his pronouncements towards the social inequalities of his time. His call for justice (Amos 5:24) echoes profoundly today as societies around the world grapple with similar issues. Many contemporary scholars and theologians have interpreted Amos as a precursor to social justice movements, emphasizing his insistence on moral integrity over ritual observance (Mays, 1969).

Moreover, Amos' condemnation of the lavish lifestyles of the elite (Amos 6:4-6) and his critique of oppression (Amos 8:4-

6) are often aligned with contemporary criticisms of economic disparity and systemic injustice. This alignment invites modern readers to draw parallels between the prophetic message and today's struggles with wealth inequality and poverty. As Alastair Hunter asserts, Amos' words "serve as a mirror reflecting the issues of our age, calling for a response" (Hunter, 1983).

Another layer of contemporary readings involves Amos' stance on religious observance. Amos challenges the authenticity of ritual practices when disconnected from ethical living (Amos 5:21-23). Today, this message resonates with those questioning the sincerity of religious observance absent of actionable compassion. As noted by Heschel, "Amos does not denounce religion per se, but rather the hypocrisy of worshipping divinely and acting unethically" (Heschel, 2001).

Furthermore, Amos' prophecies are frequently linked with the theme of accountability. He presents a deity that demands responsibility for one's actions—a concept that has found home in modern theological rhetoric. This demand mirrors contemporary calls for accountability in governance, corporate actions, and personal ethical practices. The notion that a just society must uphold accountability holds significant weight in ongoing debates over responsibility in an increasingly complex global landscape (Smith, 1995).

In reflecting on ecological ethics, Amos' foresight also finds relevance. His allusions to environmental calamities as consequences of moral failings (Amos 4:7-9) are re-examined within today's context of climate change and ecological degradation. Scholars argue that these references underscore a broader biblical mandate for environmental stewardship, positioning Amos as an early advocate for what has become an urgent, global concern (Carroll R., 2002).

Finally, contemporary readings of Amos are enriched by interfaith perspectives. Amos, who prophesied in a non-canonical setting among the Northern Kingdom, offers a voice from the margins, engaging in dialogues beyond traditional borders of faith. His universal call for justice and ethical praxis transcends religious barriers, fostering interfaith collaboration in addressing global challenges such as human rights and peacebuilding efforts (Sweeney, 1996).

In conclusion, contemporary readings of Amos reveal a prophetic text that is as much about the here and now as it is a reflection of its own time. His messages rebuke, uplift, and challenge us, urging to examine our own societal frameworks against his timeless call for justice, accountability, and authentic obedience. Understanding Amos today compels us to consider how ancient wisdom can inform and transform our world. By revisiting Amos through modern lenses, we not only honor the depth of the prophetic spirit but also engage actively with its transformative potential.

References:

Mays, J. L. (1969). *The Message of Amos*. Philadelphia: Westminster Press.
Hunter, Alastair. (1983). *Amos: His Time and His Work*. London: SCM Press.
Heschel, Abraham J. (2001). *The Prophets: Volume 1*. New York: HarperCollins.
Smith, Gary V. (1995). *Amos: A Commentary*. Louisville: Westminster John Knox Press.
Carroll R., M. Daniel (2002). *Amos—The Prophet and His Oracles: Research on the Book of Amos*. Louisville: Westminster John Knox Press.
Sweeney, Marvin A. (1996). *Prophetic Voice and Theological Expression: A Study in The Prophecies of Amos*. Michigan: Eerdmans Publishing.

Social Justice Themes in Modern Context

The modern world is characterized by an ever-growing emphasis on social justice, paralleling the hallmark concerns found within the Book of Amos. Despite being an ancient text, Amos remains remarkably contemporary, as its themes resonate with ongoing societal discourses about equity, justice, and ethical governance. It is the poignant voice of Amos, with its profound emphasis on social responsibility, that continues to echo resoundingly within today's context of humanitarian discourse.

Amos's utterances, which highlight the disparity between the rich and the poor, resonate powerfully in an era marked by stark economic inequalities. In his prophetic speech, Amos 5:24 proclaims, "But let justice roll down like waters, and righteousness like an ever-flowing stream." This instruction to pursue justice and righteousness challenges both individuals and societies to work towards a balanced and fair community where human dignity is upheld for each person, aligning with many of today's social justice movements that advocate for systemic change in issues such as income inequality, gender rights, and racial justice.

Given the burgeoning awareness and activism surrounding social justice, Amos can be interpreted as a prototypical voice for oppressed communities. The abominations perpetrated against the economically vulnerable and marginalized groups that Amos decried are still evident today. Urbanization and industrial progression have widened economic disparities, warranting renewed interaction with Amos's clarion calls for reform and advocacy against exploitation.

The ethical imperatives presented by Amos provide a framework for modern social justice that is contingent upon the execution of fair policies and altruistic leadership. Amos presents a divine repudiation of hollow religious observances that neglect the plight of the poor. His indictments against Israel's leaders can be juxtaposed with contemporary critiques of institutions that perpetuate inequality and overlook human rights. This parallel calls for an evaluative reflection within our modern systems, advocating for policies that prioritize the welfare of all citizens.

Moreover, Amos's criticism of complacency among the affluent (Amos 6:1-7) warns of the moral hazards that accompany unchecked wealth and comfort at the expense of the less fortunate. In today's world, where capital accumulation often disregards ethical considerations, these prophetic warnings serve as reminders of the responsibilities borne by those in privileged positions to utilize their influence for the common good.

Amos also challenges prevailing religious and moral paradigms, advocating for sincere worship accompanied by acts of justice and charity. His message critiques a superficial religiosity disconnected from ethical living, suggesting that authentic religious expression must involve living out justice actively. This concept urges modern believers to reconcile their faith with meaningful societal contributions, transforming worship into tangible actions for justice and peace in their communities.

Within the scope of global humanitarian work, the prophetic thrust of Amos's message has been pivotal for numerous non-profit organizations and humanitarian movements. As Oliver O'Donovan articulates in "The Desire of the Nations," the biblical motive for social justice derives from the same prophetic tradition Amos represents (O'Donovan, 1996). This prophetic legacy encourages engagement with broader social issues on a global scale, motivating individuals and institutions alike to extend the reach of justice beyond local confines.

As societies evolve under the pressures and potentials of global networks, Amos's call for justice challenges the international community to transcend regional efforts and embrace global social justice as a unified endeavor. This includes addressing the needs of displaced populations, combating human trafficking, and rectifying poverty conditions worldwide. Amos's enduring legacy inspires cross-cultural dialogues that advocate for equity, fostering a global commitment to justice as an inherent human responsibility.

In conclusion, the Book of Amos invites its interpreters to venture beyond mere textual study and engage in creating a world where justice and righteousness are living realities. As contemporary readers perceive the persistent relevance of Amos's teachings, the call to embody this prophetic vision becomes more pronounced. Today, as it did in the time of Amos, the challenge is to amplify the echoes of this ancient prophet and transform them into proactive efforts towards achieving social justice in a modern context.

References:

- O'Donovan, O. (1996). *The Desire of the Nations*. Cambridge: Cambridge University Press.

Amos and Environmental Stewardship

The prophetic writings of Amos, an ancient Hebrew prophet, continue to influence contemporary discourse in various fields, including environmental stewardship. While the primary focus of Amos was on social justice and moral transformation of society, the principles underlying his messages can be extended to the environmental concerns facing the modern world. This interpretation aligns with the broader understanding of stewardship as a fundamental biblical teaching, which involves the responsible management and care of God's creation.

The modern discourse on environmental stewardship taps into the prophetic tradition by emphasizing the interconnectedness of social, economic, and environmental justice issues. Amos's critique of the societal structures of his time resonates with today's environmental challenges, through its condemnation of the exploitation and unsustainable use of resources, which disproportionately affect the marginalized populations. As highlighted in Amos 5:24, "But let justice roll on like a river, righteousness like a never-failing stream!" (New International Version). The imagery of flowing waters as a metaphor for justice brings to the forefront the natural world's role in divine justice and wellbeing.

Amos's worldview can be seen as urging a holistic approach where justice and righteousness extend to the care of all creation. This perspective is further supported by scholars like Walter Brueggemann, who in his work *"The Prophetic Imagination"*, argues that the prophetic texts call for a transformation of society that includes ecological awareness and responsibility. According to Brueggemann, "the prophetic call is about fostering an alternative consciousness that resists the dominant injustices of the time, including the exploitation of natural resources." This alternative consciousness champions a renewed relationship with nature that recognizes the intrinsic value of all life forms.

The connection between Amos and environmental ethics also finds expressions in the Hebrew concept of "shalom," which means peace but extends to imply a harmonious existence with all elements of the earth. Amos's call for social reforms and his vision of a society where justice prevails reflect the ideals of "shalom," demanding responsibility in restoring and maintaining ecological balance. Thus, environmental stewardship becomes an extension of the justice Amos preached, a necessary component of living out the prophetic call in today's ecological crisis.

Moreover, the issue of climate change presents a modern parallel to the prophetic warnings found in Amos. As climate change continues to exacerbate global inequalities, the ethical imperatives of Amos urge a response that prioritizes justice for those most affected by environmental degradation. Scholars like Ellen F. Davis, in her book *"Scripture, Culture, and Agriculture: An Agrarian Reading of the Bible"*, argue that the ethical teachings of the Hebrew prophets, including Amos, are intrinsically linked to an agrarian ethic that respects the land and advocates for equitable resource management.

Modern applications of Amos's teachings encourage a reexamination of our current practices relating to consumption, production, and distribution of resources. Theologically, this involves viewing the earth not merely as a resource but as a sacred trust endowed to humanity by God. Responsible stewardship thus becomes a form of worship and devotion, aligning ethical choices with spiritual values centered on sustainability and protection of the earth.

The prophetic vision of Amos, when applied to environmental stewardship, challenges both individuals and institutions to engage in sustainable practices that reflect God's justice and compassion. This application requires a shift in both mindset and policy, advocating for greater creativity and commitment to ecological responsibility. By embracing Amos's call for justice as encompassing environmental ethics, we align ourselves with a tradition that recognizes caring for creation as an integral part of faithfulness to God and community.

In conclusion, the relevance of Amos in today's context extends beyond social and economic justice to include ecological responsibility. Understanding Amos through the lens of environmental stewardship enriches our interpretation of the prophetic tradition and offers a robust framework for addressing contemporary ecological challenges. By doing so, we honor the integrity of the biblical text while promoting a vision of justice that includes the flourishing of the entire creation.

Amos in Interfaith Dialogue

The dialogic encounter between the Book of Amos and today's interfaith discourse offers a profound opportunity for reflection and mutual understanding. As religious traditions grapple with modern challenges, Amos's prophetic voice serves as a bridge that encourages diverse religious communities to engage with common themes of justice, righteousness, and ethical responsibility. Recognizing shared values across faiths paves the way for a better understanding of each tradition's unique responses to contemporary issues.

Amos, a prophet from the 8th century BCE, delivered messages that transcended his immediate context to offer timeless spiritual and moral insights. Often regarded as a social justice prophet, Amos's call for justice and righteousness resonates across various religious traditions. His teachings urge adherents to confront issues of inequality, corruption, and moral decay—concerns as pertinent today as they were during his lifetime.

In interfaith dialogue, Amos becomes a compelling figure due to his commitment to principles that are echoed in different faith traditions. For instance, his emphasis on justice ("Let justice roll down like waters, and righteousness like an ever-flowing stream" - Amos 5:24) finds parallels in other sacred texts, including the Qur'an, where justice is a core tenet (Qur'an 16:90), and in the teachings of Jesus, who also urged for love and justice among humankind (Matthew 23:23). Such cross-scriptural resonances foster a shared commitment to ethical living and societal transformation.

Amos's criticisms of ritual without righteousness challenge all faiths to reflect on the authenticity of their spiritual practices and ethical commitments. His denunciation of hollow religious observance ("I hate, I despise your festivals, and I take no delight in your solemn assemblies" - Amos 5:21) encourages a sincere dialogue about the role of rituals in modern religious life. For many interfaith participants, this insight promotes discussions about how genuine faith should manifest in actionable ethics, highlighting a convergence of ideas that respects both diversity and unity.

Furthermore, Amos's messages challenge religious communities to reevaluate their responses to injustice and suffering in today's world. In an era marked by economic disparity, racial tension, and environmental challenges, the vision of Amos encourages faith groups to collaborate on common causes. Efforts such as interfaith justice coalitions, humanitarian projects, and environmental initiatives can draw inspiration from Amos's uncompromising call for social equity and ethical responsibility.

Incorporating Amos into interfaith dialogue also involves understanding his context and how it informs contemporary issues. His background as a shepherd and a farmer who spoke truth to the powerful elite demonstrates the importance of speaking out from the margins—a theme that resonates in many faiths' calls to uplift the marginalized and give voice to the voiceless. In interfaith circles, Amos becomes an exemplar of prophetic courage, inspiring communities to rise above complacency and engage in transformative action.

Amos's teachings on the relationship between power, wealth, and justice offer another dimension for interfaith engagement. His warnings to the wealthy and powerful who exploit the poor (Amos 4:1-3) provide a critical lens through which different faith communities can examine present-day power structures. Such examination fosters a collaborative approach to addressing the pressing issues of economic justice and human rights that transcend religious boundaries.

In summary, Amos serves not only as a prophetic voice from the past but as a catalyst for interfaith engagement in the present. His teachings encourage dialogue that is rooted in the shared human pursuit of dignity, justice, and divine truth. By embracing Amos's messages, interfaith dialogue can foster a profound unity that respects diversity, promotes social justice, and envisions a better future grounded in collective moral responsibility.

The Prophetic Voice of Amos in Modern Preaching

When considering the prophetic voice of Amos in the context of modern preaching, one must first appreciate the enduring relevance of his words to contemporary issues and theologically reflective discourse. Amos, an eighth-century BCE prophet, presents a model of speaking truth to power, advocating for justice and righteousness, and delivering a divine message that transcends time and culture. His role as a spokesperson for divine justice invites modern preachers to examine the themes of his prophecy and seek their application in today's world.

One of the primary reasons Amos remains a compelling prophetic voice today is his staunch emphasis on social justice. Amos calls for justice to "roll on like a river, righteousness like a never-failing stream" (Amos 5:24, NIV). This image encapsulates the urgency and perpetual nature of justice, a call that is particularly resonant in contemporary homiletic applications. Preachers today face a world rife with inequality, systemic injustice, and moral ambiguity, where religious and ethical guidance is sought more than ever. The prophetic insistence of Amos forms a foundational basis for sermons that address these issues head-on, urging congregants to adopt a proactive stance that embodies the pursuit of justice in their lived experiences.

Amos also offers an essential critique of religious ritualism devoid of ethical substance, a notion that finds its echoes in many modern religious communities. The prophet denounces empty ceremonies that lack true commitment to God's commands: "I hate, I despise your religious festivals; your assemblies are a stench to me" (Amos 5:21, NIV). This critique challenges preachers to go beyond traditional liturgical expressions and to encourage their communities to live out the principles of their faith with integrity and purpose. Engaging with Amos invites a re-evaluation of not only personal piety but the collective witness of religious communities.

Moreover, Amos's message extends an invitation to embrace a prophetic imagination, one that envisions a better world where divine justice and human action coincide. Walter Brueggemann, a noted scholar on prophetic imagination, suggests that the role of the prophet is to "offer an alternative consciousness to the dominant culture" (Brueggemann, W. "The Prophetic Imagination," Fortress Press, 1978). In this light, modern preachers are tasked with challenging the status quo, inspiring hope, and fostering transformation within their congregations. Through Amos, there is a call to move beyond complacency and into courageous proclamation of justice, mercy, and humility.

Amos's discourse on the connection between ethical living and divine favor also speaks volumes to a modern audience. He asserts that favor with God does not solely rest on religious observance but is intricately linked to social responsibility and moral actions. In Amos 5:15, he urges: "Hate evil, love good; maintain justice in the courts. Perhaps the Lord God Almighty will have mercy on the remnant of Joseph" (NIV). This ethical mandate fuels contemporary preaching that focuses on active engagement in social and political realms, advocating for rights and responsibilities that reflect godly principles.

Therefore, incorporating the prophetic voice of Amos into today's preaching requires more than rhetorical reflection; it demands profound engagement and action. It invites preachers and their communities to embrace a form of faith that is discerning, active, and persistently oriented towards justice. As preachers strive to find their own prophetic voices, Amos stands as an exemplary guide, offering both the challenge and encouragement needed to navigate and address the complexities of a modern context with authenticity and boldness.

In conclusion, Amos's prophetic contributions extend an enduring invitation to modern preachers. He challenges them to confront injustice, to call for genuine worship in spirit and truth, and to cultivate communities that embody the principles of justice and righteousness. His voice, echoing across millennia, remains a vital catalyst for change and a profound source of inspiration for those who stand to proclaim the Word in our world today.

Amos and Ethical Leadership Today

In the realm of ethical leadership, the Book of Amos provides invaluable insights that have transcended millennia, offering contemporary leaders a blueprint on moral governance and societal responsibility. The prophetic voice of Amos, steeped in a fervent call for justice and righteousness, speaks with great relevance to today's leadership challenges, addressing the critical intersection between power, morality, and societal welfare.

Amos's context was a society rife with social inequalities and exploitative leadership, much like many modern contexts. Leaders today can draw from Amos's denunciations of the injustices perpetuated by the elite in his time. His prophetic insights challenge leaders to embrace a model of ethical leadership deeply rooted in accountability and social justice. Amos chapter 5, for instance, calls for leaders to "let justice roll on like a river, righteousness like a never-failing stream" (Amos 5:24, NIV). This imagery of flowing justice emphasizes the continual and pervasive need for fairness and integrity in governance, a principle that underpins ethical leadership ideals today.

Moreover, Amos's prophecies articulate a strong rebuke against complacency among leaders who fail to uphold moral standards and the welfare of the disadvantaged. The prophet warns of inevitable consequences for those who prioritize personal gain over communal welfare. This warning remains pertinent, reminding contemporary leaders of the pitfalls of neglecting ethical responsibilities in decision-making processes.

The ethical challenges faced by modern leaders often parallel those that Amos confronted in ancient Israel. The blight of corruption, the entrenchment of social divides, and the neglect of vulnerable communities compel leaders to reconsider their role in fostering equitable and just systems. Amos's insistence on righteousness—both in personal conduct and institutional policies—serves as a guiding principle for leaders committed to cultivating organizations and societies founded on ethical ideals.

Beyond addressing systemic injustices, Amos invites today's leaders to engage in profound ethical introspection. The prophet's unwavering commitment to truth and integrity, often at great personal risk, underscores the necessity of courageous leadership. This aligns with contemporary leadership theories that emphasize authenticity and ethical behavior as critical components of effective leadership. According to Paterson and Dutcher, "Leaders who demonstrate ethical behaviors can enhance their credibility and influence, fostering a culture of trust and ethical practices within their organizations" ("Ethical Leadership in Modern Organizations," Journal of Business Ethics, 2020).

In practical terms, leaders can apply Amos's ethical teachings by embedding justice into their organizational cultures. Initiatives like transparent decision-making processes, equitable resource distribution, and inclusive dialogue reflect the ethical imperatives championed by Amos. By contextualizing his teachings into actionable strategies, leaders can foster environments where ethical considerations are prioritized, and social accountability becomes a shared value.

Furthermore, Amos's prophecies encourage an ethical leadership model that extends beyond mere compliance with legal standards. Leaders are called to align their actions with a higher moral compass, emphasizing empathy, fairness, and proactive social engagement. This prophetic emphasis on ethical leadership not only enhances organizational integrity but also contributes to broader societal transformation.

In conclusion, the Book of Amos challenges contemporary leaders to reflect deeply on their ethical responsibilities and the societal impact of their leadership. By embracing the core tenets of ethical righteousness, justice, and accountability from Amos's prophecies, leaders can navigate the complex moral landscapes of the modern world with wisdom and integrity. As the ancient prophetic voice continues to resonate through the corridors of time, it beckons leaders to enact profound change, fostering societies anchored in ethical principles and committed to the collective good.

The Influence of Amos on Contemporary Theology

The Book of Amos, a seminal text in the Hebrew Bible, continues to exert a profound influence on contemporary theology. Its enduring impact is reflected through its rich theological themes and its call for justice and righteousness, which resonate deeply in modern contexts. This underpins its perpetual relevance and its vivid interpretation in contemporary theological discourse.

One of the most compelling insights drawn from Amos is its portrayal of God as a deity intensely committed to justice. The prophet Amos courageously addresses the systemic injustices of his time, explicitly calling out the exploitation and moral decay of Israelite society. As highlighted in Amos 5:24, "But let justice roll down like waters and righteousness like an ever-flowing stream," the text emphasizes the necessity of ethical conduct as an integral part of faith. This significant motif informs contemporary theological thought, particularly in areas concerning social justice and moral integrity. The authenticity and timelessness of Amos's messages encourage theologians and religious leaders to reflect on the moral responsibilities of individuals within the broader social and economic structures.

The theme of divine sovereignty found in Amos also bears considerable weight in modern theological circles. The supreme authority of God as depicted in the prophetic oracles challenges modern believers to understand divine involvement in worldly affairs. Amos underscores the notion that God's justice is not a distant ideal but an urgent call to action within our world. Contemporary theologians often extrapolate this to understand events in the present era, fostering discussions on theodicy, divine intervention, and human responsibility.

Furthermore, Amos's emphasis on sincere worship and authentic religious practice speaks directly to current issues of religious formalism and spiritual complacency. Through Amos 5:21-23, where God rejects hollow worship observances, theologians find a critique pertinent to modern faith practices. This aspect of Amos encourages a reflective reconsideration of the purpose and depth of religious worship today, stressing the importance of aligning faith with action and ethical living.

Amos's prophetic call for social transformation remains a rallying cry within liberation theology, a movement that advocates for addressing social, political, and economic injustices. The alignment of Amos's prophetic insights with liberation theology underscores the text's persistent relevance, reinforcing its call for transformative action rooted in theological principles. As Leonardo Boff, a prominent liberation theologian, has noted, "Prophecy is disturbing because it calls all the superstructures of repression and inequity into question" (Boff, 1987). Thus, the connections between Amos and liberation theology invigorate discussions on the role of religion as a force for socio-economic equity and justice.

Additionally, environmental theologies draw from Amos's pronouncements against greed and exploitation of resources, advocating for a responsible stewardship of creation. Amos's critiques of the excesses and neglect of the poor often extend to the exploitation of the land and its resources, themes that contemporary theologies align with sustainable practices and ecological ethics. As contemporary theologians tackle issues such as climate change and environmental degradation, they often invoke Amos's voice to emphasize the ethical imperatives in addressing environmental crises.

Apart from its ethical and social implications, the Book of Amos has also influenced modern theological methods by offering a paradigm for interpreting prophetic literature. The poetic and literary techniques employed by Amos offer unique insights into the divine-human relationship, encouraging theologians to adopt a nuanced reading of sacred texts that accommodates both historical-critical and literary-theological methods. Amos invites theologians to approach the text informed by its historical context and literary artistry, achieving a comprehensive understanding that is vital in modern scriptural interpretation.

In conclusion, the influence of Amos on contemporary theology is profound and multifaceted. By addressing issues of justice, divine sovereignty, authentic worship, social transformation, and environmental stewardship, Amos speaks to a wide array of current theological discussions. The text's venerable exhortations continue to inspire and challenge modern theologians, urging them to craft a theology that is both reflective of divine justice and responsive to the exigencies of today's world. As succinctly put by Walter Brueggemann, a prominent biblical scholar, "Amos's prophetic words continue to reverberate through time, a relentless call for justice and right relationships" (Brueggemann, 2001).

Amos and Human Rights Advocacy

The Book of Amos, a cornerstone of biblical prophecy, resonates profoundly with contemporary advocacy for human rights. Although Amos prophesied in the 8th century BCE, primarily addressing the social injustices and religious hypocrisies of ancient Israel, his messages transcend time, providing a robust ethical framework for addressing modern human rights issues. Central to this discussion is Amos' unyielding call for justice and righteousness, which reverberates in the conscience of today's advocacy movements. As we delve deeper into Amos' role in human rights advocacy, we grasp how this ancient text continues to steer the moral compass of society.

In the ancient world, Amos emerged as a pioneering voice amid a culture entrenched in systemic inequality. His declarations, such as "Let justice roll down like waters, and righteousness like an ever-flowing stream" (Amos 5:24, NRSV), transcended mere rhetoric to become a profound moral imperative. Amos confronted the societal structures of his day, critiquing the economic exploitation and legal injustices that plagued the marginalized. This critique is eerily reminiscent of modern struggles against systemic oppression, suggesting that the human rights issues of our time are not entirely new but rather iterations of age-old conflicts.

Amos' advocacy for the poor and disenfranchised establishes him not only as a religious leader but also as a proto-human rights activist. His vivid imagery and bold pronouncements challenge us to reevaluate the priorities of society. The prophet's insistence on fairness calls into question legal systems and societal norms that perpetuate inequality. In the eyes of Amos, divine justice encompasses not just spiritual integrity but social and economic equitableness, offering a holistic vision of societal transformation.

The relevance of Amos in contemporary human rights advocacy is further highlighted by the shared themes between his prophecies and modern international human rights documents, such as the Universal Declaration of Human Rights. Both emphasize the inviolability of human dignity and the fundamental right to justice. Moreover, Amos provides a theological rationale for human dignity, asserting that societal ills are not merely legal transgressions but violations against the divine order, thereby reinforcing the intrinsic value of every human being.

Institutions and movements today draw upon Amos' message to inspire action and articulate the moral imperatives of their causes. His critique of opulence at the expense of the impoverished finds echoes in the advocacy for economic justice pursued by organizations such as Amnesty International and Human Rights Watch. These groups echo Amos' passionate denunciations by holding nations accountable for their failure to uphold human rights standards.

Furthermore, Amos' standpoint on accountability profoundly impacts contemporary discourse around corporate responsibility and governmental transparency. His prophecies encourage a proactive stance toward ethical stewardship, compelling leaders to pursue policies that promote the common good. Recent movements toward corporate social responsibility (CSR) in multinational organizations can be seen as a modern reincarnation of Amos' clarion call for accountability and moral governance.

Interfaith dialogues centered on justice and human rights often invoke Amos' teachings, fostering a collective responsibility to address global injustices. Such dialogues not only bridge theological divides but fortify a shared commitment towards humanitarian goals, driven by Amos' universal message of justice as the thread binding varied cultural and religious narratives.

Lastly, the timeless wisdom of Amos finds fertile ground in educational programs that aim to nurture ethical leadership. His insights are incorporated into curricula aimed at instilling values of equity and justice among future leaders. By integrating Amosian principles into the fabric of leadership training, today's educational initiatives aim to cultivate leaders who are capable of addressing the complex human rights challenges of the 21st century.

In conclusion, the Book of Amos stands as a pivotal resource in the arena of human rights advocacy. As his messages echo through the ages, they challenge us to engage courageously with the injustices of our world and affirm the sacred duty to uphold the dignity and rights of every individual. Through Amos' prophetic vision, we discern a timeless blueprint for justice, empowering us toward the realization of a more equitable and compassionate world.

Reinterpreting Amos in the Digital Age

As we delve into the intricate relationship between the prophetic messages of the Book of Amos and the rapidly evolving dynamics of the digital age, it becomes imperative to explore how ancient scriptures can be reinterpreted and recontextualized to offer insights into our current technological landscape. The emergence of digital platforms has not only transformed communication but has significantly shaped our socio-political environment. Therefore, understanding how Amos's messages can be remolded in these contexts could offer profound insights into their relevance today.

Amos, renowned for his unyielding stance on social justice and ethical conduct, primarily focused on addressing the disparities and the moral decadence of his time. Today, these fundamental themes resonate with the ongoing discussions surrounding digital ethics and online conduct. In the era of social media, where the dissemination of information is rapid and widespread, the prophetic voice of Amos calls upon individuals and communities to exercise accountability, integrity, and truthfulness in digital interactions. Through the lens of Amos, we are invited to assess whether our digital behaviors uphold the principles of equity and justice, reminiscent of his exhortations against falsehood and exploitation in ancient Israel.

The digital age also presents a platform for amplifying messages of justice and equity, akin to Amos's persistent advocacy against societal injustices. The accessibility and reach afforded by digital tools empower advocates and leaders to echo Amos-like calls for social reform. However, this amplification comes with an obligation to maintain authenticity and avoid the entrapments of performative activism. The prophet reminds us that true justice extends beyond appearances and requires tangible action, a principle that can guide contemporary digital activism efforts.

Further, digital platforms have cultivated environments where misinformation can propagate, challenging the fabric of truth that Amos so fervently defended. In Amos 5:10-15, the prophet's critique of the judicial system reflects his disdain for the subversion of truth, a message that finds relevance today as societies grapple with the proliferation of fake news and disinformation online. In reinterpreting Amos's exhortation of maintaining justice, current efforts can focus on ensuring transparency and promoting factual accuracy in digital communications, thereby embodying the prophet's vision for a society anchored on ethical integrity.

Moreover, the digital age's accelerated information sharing encourages dialogues that bridge diverse communities, aligning with the interfaith discussions inspired by Amos's messages. The digital world, when used positively, can be a conduit for mutual understanding and respect among varied beliefs and cultures, facilitating dialogues that Amos would endorse. His universal messages of equality and moral righteousness apply to broader global conversations, and in cyberspace, are enhanced by cross-cultural platforms that allow for rich exchanges of ideas and beliefs.

Reinterpreting Amos in the digital age also means addressing the environmental concerns that echo the prophet's themes of stewardship and responsibility. As digital platforms highlight ecological crises, they can serve to mobilize collective action towards environmental justice. Amos's admonitions serve as a poignant reminder of our duty as caretakers of the earth, urging a protective stance against wanton digital resource exploitation and the ensuing environmental degradation.

In conclusion, the prophetic insights of Amos, when viewed through the prism of the digital age, promote a reconsideration of our ethical frameworks and stewardship roles. As technology continues to transform society, the lessons of Amos regarding truth, justice, and communal responsibility provide a timeless beacon of guidance. The digital age is not only a period of substantial challenge but also a realm of opportunity to embody and disseminate the enduring messages of Amos effectively and meaningfully.

This reimagining of Amos encourages us to harness digital tools not only as instruments of communication but as platforms for fostering an equitable and just global community, a vision that Amos himself would undoubtedly advocate.

Amos and Global Poverty: A Modern Perspective

In the backdrop of a rapidly globalizing world, the ancient prophecies of Amos resonate profoundly, particularly when addressing the persistent and pervasive issue of global poverty. Amos, the herdsman from Tekoa, stands as a torchbearer of social justice, crying out against economic disparities and exploitation. His ancient words provide a glaringly relevant lens through which we can examine and critique the poverty endemic to our modern sociopolitical landscapes. Similarly, the stark calls for justice in Amos provide impetus and direction for contemporary efforts aimed at poverty alleviation.

Poverty transcends geographical boundaries, affecting billions worldwide. According to the World Bank, as of the recent statistics, nearly 10% of the world's population lives on less than $1.90 a day—markers of extreme poverty limit access to basic needs. This echoes Amos's era, where disparities were marked between the affluent urban dwellers and the impoverished rural communities (cf. Amos 6:1-6). The prophet's unyielding censure of those "who lie on beds of ivory" while the poor are trampled upon (Amos 6:4) is a testament to the timeless nature of economic inequalities.

Amos's visions and oracles are fundamentally anchored in the ethical and theologized fabric of justice. His admonishments highlight the moral failing of hoarding wealth at the expense of the marginalized. In the twenty-first century, where the chasm between wealth and poverty continues to widen, Amos serves as a pivotal voice in advocating for equitable wealth distribution. Modern monetary policies and international aid efforts can draw from Amos—inspiring strategies that prioritize upliftment from poverty over profit maximization.

In an era of burgeoning technology and unprecedented interconnectedness, the digital divide highlights another dimension of modern poverty. Access to technology, or the lack thereof, significantly influences one's economic prospects. Much like the biblical era inequities, contemporary access to resources is starkly uneven. Amos's denunciation of exploitation and neglect of the poor could well extend to digital disenfranchisement, challenging the affluent to ensure access to technology is justly distributed.

The prophetic call of Amos extends beyond mere denunciation of existing inequities; it also implores transformative actions. Amos 5:24—"But let justice roll on like a river, righteousness like a never-failing stream!"—offers not just a vivid metaphor but an actionable blueprint for social reform. Contemporary policymakers, non-profit organizations, and advocacy groups are tasked with creating mechanisms that ensure fair distribution and access to wealth, resources, and opportunities.

Furthermore, ecological degradation often exacerbates poverty, a scenario where Amos's recognition of justice connects with environmental causes. Poor communities are disproportionately affected by environmental catastrophes, a situation reminiscent of ancient Israel's exploitation of natural resources. Amos's equitable vision for society can propel modern environmental stewardship, aligning ecological health with poverty alleviation as dual goals that are interdependent.

In engaging with global poverty, the interreligious dimension emerges as a poignant parallel to Amos's message. Religious communities worldwide, drawing inspiration from Amos's call to justice, can act collaboratively against poverty. This transcends doctrinal boundaries, creating a coalition of faith-led initiatives focused on eradicating poverty through shared resources, advocacy, and grassroots mobilizations.

The application of Amos to contemporary poverty issues thus transcends mere theological study—it moves into action-oriented discourse. Seminaries, congregational leaders, and community activists can employ the prophetic themes of Amos within educational contexts, conversations, and campaigns directed at poverty eradication. By revisiting Amos, educators can inspire a generation that values justice as intrinsic to societal well-being.

In summary, the specter of global poverty finds a formidable adversary in the prophetic declarations of Amos. His relentless pursuit of justice, equity, and community welfare beckons modern societies not just to reinterpret, but to actively embody his ideals in solutions tailored to eradicate poverty. Amos's message serves as both a critical lens and a motivating mandate for those seeking to transform his visionary call into persistent realities for today's world.

www.ingramcontent.com/pod-product-compliance
Lightning Source LLC
LaVergne TN
LVHW051144250125
802145LV00008B/431